fermata

For Ono,

companion in a lifetime of music listening,

for Stephanie Gibbons,

and all friends who tune the way.

fermata friends

The publication of *fermata* was made possible by the many generous contributions donated so kindly to our *Fund it* campaign.

We thank you all sincerely for this support, it was most encouraging and greatly appreciated.

We particularly wish to acknowledge the sponsorship of the following:

Dr Eoin Bourke, Galway

John Carney, Dublin

Connemara Carpets Ltd., Moyard, Co Galway *www.connemaracarpets.com*

Conamara Environmental Education & Cultural Centre, Letterfrack, Co. Galway *www.ceecc.org*

Henry Glassie and John McGuigan, Bloomington, Indiana

Dr Hans Hüebner, Munich

Joan & Joe McBreen, Galway

James Joyce Whiskey, James Joyce House, 15 Usher's Island, Dublin 8 *www.jamesjoycewhiskey.ie*

Daniel Rosen, Galway

First published in Ireland 2016
by Artisan House Limited
Letterfrack, Connemara
Co Galway, Ireland

Editors	**Eva Bourke** and **Vincent Woods**
Foreword	**Mícheál Ó Súilleabháin**
Editorial Director	**Mary Ruddy**
Creative Director	**Vincent Murphy**
Illustrations	**Miriam de Búrca**
Photography	**Christy McNamara**
Printing	**Imago** Slovenia

See detailed photography and illustration credits on page 270

ISBN **978 0 9926908 8 5**

A CIP catalogue record for this book is available from the British Library.

Paper used in the production of this title is made from wood grown in sustainable forests.

fermata

Writings inspired by Music

Edited by Eva Bourke and Vincent Woods

Foreword by

Professor Mícheál Ó Súilleabháin

ARTISAN HOUSE PUBLISHING

Books of *taste* Created with *passion* In the heart of *Connemara*

www.artisanhouse.ie

CONTENTS

Mícheál **Ó Súilleabháin** *Fermata – A Poetic Moment* 8
Eva **Bourke** and Vincent **Woods** *Articulated Light – Word to Music* 14

I Songbirds in the Stairwell

John **Montague** *Hearth Song* 28, *Windharp* 29
Michael **Longley** *The Stairwell* 30
Seamus **Heaney** *The Canopy* 31
Eamon **Grennan** *Untitled* 32
Vona **Groarke** *The Garden as Music and Silence* 33
Chris **Agee** *The nightingales* 34
Pearse **Hutchinson** *A Findrum Blackbird* 35
Thomas **Kinsella** *Song of the Night – Philadelphia, Carraroe* 36
Mary **O'Malley** *Geography* 39
David **Wheatley** *Klangfarbenmelodie* 40
Kerry **Hardie** *Leaf-Fall* 41
Matthew **Sweeney** *The Canary* 42
Moya **Cannon** *Song in Windsor, Ontario* 43
Michael **O'Dea** *The Green Road* 44
Eva **Bourke** *Swallows* 45
Alice **Lyons** *marram* 46
Joseph **Woods** *Singing Gate* 48
Peter **Fallon** *Home from Home* 49
Maurice **Riordan** *Faun Whistling to a Blackbird* 49
Dermot **Healy** *The Litany of the Wagtail* 50
Gabriel **Rosenstock** *Young Gypsy Musician* 52

II The Given Note

Seamus **Heaney** *The Given Note* 56
John F **Deane** *The Upright Piano* 57
Mark **Granier** *Vulture Bone Flute* 58
Vona **Groarke** *Interval* 59
Eamon **Grennan** *Kate Singing* 60
Matthew **Sweeney** *Do Wah Diddy Diddy Do* 61
Louis **de Paor** *Didjeridu* 62, 63
Annie **Deppe** *The Throat Singers* 64
Rita Ann **Higgins** *She's Easy* 66
Peter **Fallon** *Sean Nós* 67
Theo **Dorgan** *Singer #6* 68, *Singer #62* 69
Gerard **Hanberry** *Lilter* 70
Ciaran **O'Driscoll** *Catch* 71
Pearse **Hutchinson** *Pibroch* 72

Mary **O'Malley** *Footsteps* 73
Michael **Longley** *Fleadh* 74
Thomas **McCarthy** *Bel Canto* 76
Derek **Mahon** *The Andean Flute* 77
Mary **Noonan** *The Fado House of Argentina Santos* 78
Pearse **Hutchinson** *The Miracle of Bread and Fiddles* 79
James **Joyce** *Lean out of the window* 80
Tar go dtí an fhuinneog *trans. Gabriel Rosenstock* 81
Peter **Sirr** *Three Poems* 82
Pat **Boran** *Concert off Kensington High Street* 86
Jan **Wagner** *giovanni gnocchi plays the cello* *trans. Eva Bourke* 87
Hugo **Hamilton** excerpt from *Disguise* 88
Gerard **Smyth** *Little Mysteries* 90
Enda **Wyley** *Cúil Aodha Singer* 91
Pat **Boran** *Guitar* 92
Eugene **O'Connell** *Blind Faith* 93
Pete **Mullineaux** *A Piper Prepares* 95

III A Sad Air's Best for Night

Eiléan **Ní Chuilleanáin** *Hofstetter's Serenade* 98
Chris **Agee** *Nine years* 99
Louis **de Paor** *Rory* 100, 101
Paul **Durcan** *In Memory: The Miami Showband – Massacred 31 July 1975* 102
Pearse **Hutchinson** *Ó Riada* 103
Leland **Bardwell** *Outside the Odeon, Camden Town* 104, *Insomnia* 105
Michael **Longley** *Words for Jazz Perhaps* 106
Macdara **Woods** *Salt Fields* 108
Hugh **Maxton** *War and Music* 109
Paula **Meehan** *Home* 110
Geraldine **Mitchell** *Grief* 112
John **Montague** *Lullaby* 113
Leanne **O'Sullivan** *In Your Sleep* 114
Dennis **O'Driscoll** *Nocturne, Op. 2* 115
Moya **Cannon** *Lament* 116
Colm **Tóibín** excerpt from *Everything is Susceptible* 117
Michael **Longley** *Madame Butterfly* 120
Thomas **McCarthy** *Scriabin's Piano Sonata No. 2 in G sharp minor, Op. 19* 121
Eva **Bourke** *The Irish Tenor Michael Kelly Recalls Mozart in Paris* 122
Ted **Deppe** *The Funeral March of Adolf Wölfli* 124
Eugene **O'Connell** *Letters from Africa* 126 , *On the Pier* 126
Julie **O'Callaghan** *Saturday Afternoon in Dublin* 127
John **McAuliffe** *At a Concert* 128
David **Wheatley** from *Sonnets to Robert Fergusson (1750–1774)* 129
Martina **Evans** *Burnfort, Las Vegas,* 130, *Elvis is Dying* 131
Ken **Bruen** *To Have To Hold* 132

Michael **O'Dea** *Those Marches* 139
Sinéad **Morrissey** *The Evil Key* 140
Matthew **Sweeney** *Into the Air* 142
Leontia **Flynn** *Country Songs* 143
Dermot **Bolger** *The Piper Patsy Touhey Plays in Cohen's Variety Show, New York, 1905* 144
Mary **Noonan** *Hi-Lili Hi-Lo* 145
Kathleen **McCracken** *A Minor* 146
Enda **Wyley** *Orpheus Speaks* 147

IV Girl in a Wheelchair Dancing

John F **Deane** *Canticle* 150
Dennis **O'Driscoll** *The Good Old Days* 151
Macdara **Woods** *My Degas Words* 152
Pat **Boran** *Master* 153, *Young Master* 153
Mark **Granier** *Girl in a Wheelchair Dancing to U2* 154
James **Harpur** *Jubilate* 155
Leontia **Flynn** *By My Skin* 156
Moya **Cannon** *'Songs last the longest...'* 157
Paddy **Bushe** *Music Lesson, Xiahe* 158
Emmanuel **Jakpa** *Tales* 159
Vona **Groarke** *Music from Home* 160
John **McAuliffe** *Continuity* 161
Derek **Mahon** *Morning Radio* 162
Paula **Meehan** *Two Buck Tim from Timbuctoo* 163
Seamus **Heaney** *The Rain Stick* 164
Jan **Wagner** *hippocampus* *trans. Eva Bourke* 165
Julie **O'Callaghan** *Misty Island* 166
Mary **O'Malley** *Tory* 167
Ciaran **O'Driscoll** *Wasps in the Session* 168
Kathleen **McCracken** *Corn and Cockcrow* 169
Vincent **Woods** *The Green Fields of Vietnam* 170
Theo **Dorgan** *Singer #15* 172, *Singer #17* 173
Geraldine **Mitchell** *Basso Continuo* 174
Peter **Fallon** from *Ballynahinch Postcards* 175
Medbh **McGuckian** *Novena* 176
Moya **Cannon** *Night Road in the Mountain* 177

V Three Men Standing at the Met

Michael **Coady** *Three Men Standing at the Met* 180
Dermot **Bolger** *Séamus Ennis in Drumcondra* 188
Paul **Durcan** *My Mother's Secret* 189
Joan **McBreen** *On Hearing My Daughter Play 'The Swan'* 190
Kathleen **McCracken** *How Old Is Ian Tyson?* 191

Mary **Noonan** *But I should Never Think of Spring* 192
Leontia **Flynn** *The Yanks* 193
Tom **French** *Like Cherry Flakes Falling* 194
John F **Deane** *Brief History of a Life* 199
James **Harpur** *Opera* 200
Iggy **McGovern** *The Choir* 201
Mark **Granier** *The Mock Leaving* 202
Michael **Longley** *Harmonica* 203
Peter **Woods** excerpt from *The Living Note* 204
Rachel **McNicholl** *Breezie in the Organ Loft* 208
Rita Ann **Higgins** *The Faraways* 211
Gerard **Smyth** from *Dancing in the Attic* 214, *Ship in the Night* 215
Brian **Leyden** excerpt from *Last Night's Dancing* 216
John **McAuliffe** *Effects* 218
Jan **Wagner** *the études* *trans. Eva Bourke* 219
John **Montague** *The Family Piano* 220
Justin **Quinn** *Night Songs* 221
Derek **Mahon** *Rock Music* 224
Eiléan **Ní Chuilleanáin** *The Percussion Version* 225
Medbh **McGuckian** *Blue Kasina* 226
Catherine P **MacCarthy** from *Land League Cottage, i Nocturne* 228, *iii Orfeo* 229

VI Listening to Bach

Kerry **Hardie** *Musician* 232
Harry **Clifton** *To the Korean Composer Song-On Cho* 233
Caitríona **O'Reilly** *The Swan Theme* 235
Ciaran **Carson** excerpt from *Last Night's Fun* 236
John F **Deane** *Death Lullaby* 240
Vincent **Woods** *McKenna's Tunes* 241
Deirdre **Cronin** *No Strings Attached* 242
David **Wheatley** *The Treasures of a Folklore Beyond Compare* 246, *White Nights* 247
Paddy **Bushe** *Cloisfead Ar Neamh* 248, *I Shall Hear in Heaven* 248
Eva **Bourke** *Riddle Canon* 249
Gerard **Hanberry** *Listening to Townes Van Zandt* 250, *The Rocker* 251
Joseph **Woods** *House-Sitting to Chet Baker* 252
Thomas **McCarthy** *Listening to Lera Auerbach* 253
John **Sheahan** *Ronnie's Heaven* 254
Dermot **Healy** *Somerset Maugham on Bass with the Harp Jazz Band in Enniskillen* 256
Sinéad **Morrissey** *Shostakovich* 258
Pearse **Hutchinson** *Listening to Bach* 259

Acknowledgements 260
Index 266
Profiles 271

Fermata – A poetic moment   Mícheál Ó Súilleabháin

Several decades ago I was in a West Cork recording studio editing and mixing music I had just recorded with the Irish Chamber Orchestra. The recording engineer, Tadhg Kelleher, was using the new Pro Tools audio software programme for editing digital sound, and this was one of my earliest exposures to the wonders of the relatively new digital technology.

At one point the piano and orchestra moved towards a paused chord – the notational device to indicate this is a fermata:

At such a point in the music, the performers must hold the note and stop any metrical measurement of musical time until the conductor or director indicates the reinstatement of the meter. The effect can be extraordinary. If the conductor holds for too long, a point rapidly comes when the tension in the music starts to lose power and the effect is one of anti-climax. If the hold is too short, there can be a sense of disappointment at an emotional opportunity lost. If metrical counting has been suspended, how is such a hold measured? Perhaps it might be possible to describe the hold as being more spatially than metrically measured. Consider this: you are at the edge of a cliff and your task is to leap across a void onto a safe landing-place opposite you. You must land firmly on your feet as onto a moving train and pick up the same speed you had as you came to the edge of the cliff. How to judge the gap is the question. Too short a leap will have you dashed on the rocks below. Too long a leap will have you flat on your face trying to get back up to your former speed before the holding exercise.

This is a fermata in music, a magic moment when in certain instances there is an enormous build up of tension – often accompanied by an increase in the dynamics: in other words a progressive increase in volume tracked to the non-metrical duration of the fermata creates a combined effect of a great surge of emotion.

There are, however, other uses of the fermata in music. For example, a fermata on the very final notes or chord of a piece accompanied by a decrease in dynamics creates the feeling of being gently brought back down to ground in a gentle but firm gesture of letting go.

At any rate, in the studio the time had arrived to play back the edited section. Immediately I noticed something was 'missing'. The tension that had been in the held chord – the one with the fermata sign over it – had simply disappeared! I queried that and was astonished to find that a small number of milliseconds had been lopped off the held chord in the process of making the edit that joined that chord to the next chord and thus reintroducing the metrical count. The result was that of an anti-climax. It seems that in making music, we feel in milliseconds – and this becomes apparent in a dramatic way when we are called upon to 'feel' rather than count the pure duration of a fermata moment.

It is as if there is a pure durational existence behind the artificial metrical skeleton of the music. If the regular – or irregular – grouping of beats within a metrical framework provides the engine that makes the music run and the feet tap, then the actual momentum may be generated by something more 'off the ground', something uplifted and thrown into the air.

'Laudate Dominum' from *Graduale Triplex* (Abbaye Saint-Pierre de Solesmes: Solesmes 1973, p.664)

There are many non-metrical music traditions across world cultures. Frequently these are associated with spiritual music. The best Western example is Gregorian Chant where the momentum of the sung line is so held aloft through the relative duration of notes that the tradition has firmly resisted any attempt to modernise the music notation system used. Instead of the international usage of a five-line stave, the medieval four-line stave is used along with a series of unmeasured note heads that avoid the stems that would indicate predictable metrical patterns. The example of chant notation also includes examples of the original neumes (early musical notation dating from 9th and 10th centuries) above and below the four-line stave.

There are various theories around the emergence of these neumes – some that claim their origins lie in hand gestures indicating the movement and sweep of the sung line, others claim their origins in punctuation.

It is at this level of the visual sign that allows an initial bridge into poetry – the full stop, the comma, the colon, the semi-colon, the hyphen, the italic, the bold, the apostrophe, quotation marks, lineation, punctuation, and pagination. Some signs tell us to slow down slightly (*poco rit* in music notation), others draw us up sharply and expectantly as in a colon: perhaps a musical equivalent might be a sudden measured short silence serving to focus the attention on what is to follow.

The metrical foot in poetry (the meter in musical terms) sets up clearly identifiable rhythms through the trochee, iamb, spondee, dactyl, anapaest, and amphimacer. Tempo in music (the speed of a piece) has somatic equivalents in such terms as *andante* (at a walking pace). The idea of a metrical foot, therefore, has both the music and the words literally dancing. The rise and fall of the hand gestures that produced the neumes (durational moments beneath and beyond meter), along with the rhythmic foot movements that measure the line across the earth, set up a movement between the earth and the heavens redolent of Heaney's lovely injunction:

We should keep our feet on the ground to signify that nothing is beneath us, and we should also lift up our eyes so that nothing is beyond us.

There are of course shared words between music and poetry with equivalent meanings: a phrase of music is a segment perceived as a subsection of a longer musical strain that is sometimes termed a sentence. And that word 'strain' also claims our attention in that it has a long history of being used in music – perhaps especially in song. The strain in the tightening of the larynx in order to produce a singing sound has been suggested as a source for this usage. The movement of a looser prosaic speech into the more heightened intonations of performed poetry involves a somatic transformation akin to singing to a greater or lesser extent. Yeats's 1930s BBC poetry broadcasts, in what Heaney called 'elevated chanting' and what Nick Laird has described as a 'kind of quavery shamanic intoning – as if summoning demons' – go as far as to raise the voice to a clearly identifiable monotone of more or less fixed pitch.

Interestingly, we also find a movement crossing from the opposite side of the equation. Coinciding with Yeats's earlier 'elevated chanting' is the *Sprechgesang* (spoken singing) of Wagnerian opera where recitative wins the day. Or, more dramatically, the *Sprechstimme* of Schoenberg's *Pierrot Lunaire* (1912) where the constant pitch maintained throughout a note is immediately abandoned by falling or rising.

But let me end with two poetic examples of another kind of fermata or holding in poetry. These are heroic moments of apostrophe when speech is heightened and the absolute soundlessness of the drawing of the veil of the temple, of penetrating the iconostasis, reveals the presence of another side.

This moment of epiphany is just long enough for us to sense what is in the offing, and short enough to leave us down again into mystery. When it is revealed in poetry there is a moment when the image is caught for all time, to be revisited like an iconic window into light.

Thus, Heaney's *The Pitchfork* serves as a tuning fork as he speaks of it to Dennis O'Driscoll in *Stepping Stones: Interviews with Seamus Heaney*:

> *Tasty work, as they say. Using the pitchfork was like playing an instrument. So much so that when you clipped and trimmed the head of a ruck, the strike of the fork on the hay made it a kind of tuning fork.*

The bell-like strike of the fork sends the image startlingly and magically into the air in a held fermata moment:

And when he thought of probes that reached the farthest,
He would see the shaft of a pitchfork sailing past
Evenly, imperturbably through space,
Its prongs starlit and absolutely soundless –

But has learned at last to follow that simple lead
Past its own aim, out to an other side
Where perfection – or nearness to it – is imagined
Not in the aiming but the opening hand.

The opening hand that releases the moment is the gestural neume of pure duration. It is analogous to whatever visual sign denotes the movement of the pitchfork as javelin in free-fall through the air. The flying pitchfork is caught in a kinetic fermata through its relationship between the object in motion and the opened hand. Kinetics in classical mechanics is also termed dynamics – the same term used in music to denote the sense of motion created through an increase or decrease in amplitude.

We have already noted the relationship between a held sound and its changing amplitude. The ping of the pitchfork has set off a weightless moment in the poem through a perfectly timed strain of tension, imagery and sonic integrity.

Another great fermata moment of held suspension comes at the very end of Philip Larkin's *The Whitsun Weddings:*

and it was nearly done, this frail
Travelling coincidence; and what it held
Stood ready to be loosed with all the power
That being changed can give. We slowed again,
And as the tightened brakes took hold, there swelled
A sense of falling, like an arrow-shower
Sent out of sight, somewhere becoming rain.

Larkin wrote in advance of a BBC broadcast of the poem: 'I might just add a note about its reading: it is pitched if anything in an even lower key than usual… success or failure of the poem depends on whether it gets off the ground on the last two lines'.

The powerful transformative effect of the train slowing towards a held moment of brake sparks creates a sense of swelling – a combination of *deaccelerando* and *crescendo* (increasing amplitude) releases a final adrenalin rush of an arrow-shower where Larkin's 'Sent out of sight, somewhere' is akin to Heaney's 'out to an other side'.

Vincent Woods and Eva Bourke in this collection of writings have pitched music into the heart of things. From Seamus Heaney to John Montague, Eiléan Ní Chuilleanáin to Mary O'Malley, Pearse Hutchinson to Louis de Paor, a kaleidoscope of sounds is evoked from 'songbirds circling high in the staircase' to 'bits of a tune / Coming in on loud weather'. With Rita Ann Higgins, Moya Cannon, Michael Longley, Thomas Kinsella, and a wide mix of other writers we range across Inuit throat singing, sean-nós, lilting, pibroch, bel canto, birdsong, fado, jazz, country songs, nocturnes, and marches. Musicians are invoked and remembered: Shostakovich, Lera Auerbach, Seán Ó Riada, Gabriel Fauré, Bach, Rory Gallagher, the Miami Showband. It is as if it is all caught within Heaney's upended Rain Stick where 'You are like a rich man entering heaven / Through the ear of a raindrop. Listen now again'.

We have long believed that poetry and music are deeply connected art forms. Since first meeting in Galway through the poetry and music events organised there in the early 1980s, we have explored and celebrated music in our own writing as well as through many events and public performances we organised with writers, musicians and singers. A strong spirit of connection between music and word is an essential and enduring element of Irish literary and musical traditions, and since the 1960s new generations of poets and prose writers have explored and honoured music in their work and performance, with many musicians and composers likewise finding inspiration in the written word.

The shadows of Yeats and Joyce are frequently invoked in reference to Irish literary life and impulses. Their love of music and interweaving of song and music in their poems, plays and novels have undoubtedly inspired many writers. But they were drawing on an older tradition while making the new, and countless writers since then have made their own bright shadows out of the heart and chords of music, renewed the old and made new, original, invigorating work that holds the pulse, the *cuisle* of heard and given notes.

In the course of some now-hazy conversation, we realised that there was no compilation or anthology of contemporary Irish writing on music. Inspired in part by 'Lines of Vision: Irish Writers on Art', edited by Janet McLean and published by the National Gallery of Ireland, we decided to set to work on making a book that would bring together some of the many and diverse writings we have heard and read on the infinite themes of music and its variations.

We considered confining our remit to poetry, then decided we should expand it to include at least some of the prose writers who have drawn on music and added to it in their work. We made a list of names, sent out emails, trawled in collections of poetry and prose, despaired at our omissions, and took heart from the generous response we received from so many writers. Then with our publishers, Artisan House, we ran a *Fund it* campaign to raise the money for publication, commissioned original artwork from Miriam de Búrca, sifted and sorted and eventually settled on a shape and title for our book. We considered many options for a title and finally agreed on *fermata*, a term Mícheál Ó Súilleabháin explains with great elegance and insight in his foreword to this book. The writing, when assembled and read over many times, fell naturally into different categories: sound and music from nature; source and transformation; elegy and lament; celebration; music as memory and testament; and the honouring of composers and music-makers. Some writing crosses boundaries of definition and category, as the best music does, but we believe that all of it is marked by a passionate act of listening transformed, of sound reimagined into the shape of words, of one art form striving to honour another.

The first chapter, 'Songbirds in the Stairwell', is a close listening to the multiple soundtracks of nature. In Seamus Heaney's poem 'Canopy', the poet describes a miraculous transformation of an ordinary May afternoon in the leafy grounds of Harvard Yard brought about by loudspeakers wrapped in sacking and installed in the tree branches, looking like 'old wasps' nests' and transmitting 'speech-gutterings'. This chorus from the tree branches almost but not quite produces music; it is a preliminary stage to choral singing, making use of musical elements like sound, voice, dynamics, volume, speed and rhythm. The poet artfully makes us 'hear' the 'whispering wood' and eventually the reader seems to share a space with the Harvard listeners who feel startled, surrounded by a confusion of disembodied voices. 'People were cocking their ears, / Gathering, quietening, / Stepping into the grass, / stopping and holding hands.' But it works both ways: not only are words 'being given new airs', but also airs are given new words, reaching the ear and working their transformational magic in the listeners' minds.

Much that has been written on the relationship between music and language makes their affinity explicit, while other writing points out their profound differences. The transmissions from the voice boxes in the trees of Harvard Yard are not classifiable as either music or language, but they constitute organised sound which is perhaps intentionally close to musical as well as natural sound. Heaney compares it to phenomena like 'ebb and flow, hush and backwash', and to 'antiphonal responses in the congregation of leaves'. There is a paradox inherent in this – natural sound is neither language nor music, yet it is, according to the poet, capable of transporting an undercurrent of meaning. In this poem it is clearly a redemptive message: 'the wood of the suicides – / Had been magicked to lover's lane'.

The German philosopher, composer and musical theorist Theodor W Adorno has said that music is similar to but not identical with language. Their close relationship is immediately obvious: both are directed at the human ear, and both rely on a system of symbolical signs on the page. Another analogy is that both language and music take place in a linear temporal space. But whereas language can convey a clear message, music remains allusive, or connotative. The natural musical sounds of our environment, on the other hand, are akin to but not the same as either music or language: they are non-referential, and the way they communicate meaning depends entirely on the individual listener's interpretation. The same nightingale can be deeply mournful to one listener and mellifluously consoling to another. The cricket in the Nialls' cottage, for example, in John Montague's poem 'Hearth Song', 'that minute, manic cellist', sings to the young boy 'a hearth song of happiness'. The poet, zooming out of the microcosm of the insect in one sweeping movement to an almost cosmic vantage point, compares the cricket's 'solitary, compulsive song' to 'earth's fragile, atonal rhythm'. There is method in this, and it recurs throughout this chapter: the sonorous percussive tones and 'long horn call blown off the ocean', the 'inner ear roar' of the sea in Kinsella's 'Song of the Night', or the 'rapt cacophony' and 'soul hymnal' of starlings in a sycamore in Eamon Grennan's poem 'Untitled', or the atonal sound music overheard near a lake by Humber in David Wheatley's experimental 'Klangfarbenmelodie', orchestrated by a whole zoo of water fowl and lake-side dwellers, all these choruses and cellists, percussionists, flautists, singers and oboists push open doors beyond our humdrum existence into a separate and imaginary ideal realm where music reigns supreme.

This, of course, is an entirely subjective reaction and open to dispute – but then all interpretation of music, including the 'music' of nature, must be subjective, since music is non-directive: it pursues nothing and leaves it entirely up to us what we ourselves might bring to or take from it. In some instances in the first chapter this is taken a step further by a synaesthetic sleight of hand. In Pearse Hutchinson's 'A Findrum Blackbird', the bird's song turns the front garden into a glade-scriptorium with 'black-and-yellow music'. The delight Dermot Healy derived from watching a wagtail trip and flit to and fro is expressed so vividly in the brisk beat and short lines of the poem that abound with onomatopoeia, or 'sound painting', that one can hear the flutter of wings and feel the air stirred by the small bird's 'bounce of brightness, / chase down-the-wind.' Alice Lyons's 'marram' is a graceful visual as well as a Joycean word-music poem. The robin on a skeletal hawthorn in 'Green Road' by Michael O'Dea sings notes that singe the February air. In Maurice Riordan's engaging 'Faun Whistling to a Blackbird', the faun is rewarded for his troubles by the bird replying with 'some Goidelic curse' it had picked up 'beside the Erne or Belfast Lough'. The chapter concludes with one of Gabriel Rosenstock's ekphrastic haiku in which the poet merges music and image with the three-line poem in four different languages. The young gypsy musician travelling the long road with his cello on his back is the embodiment of the artist constantly in search of patrons – he seems enviably free, but his freedom comes at a high price.

In chapter two, 'The Given Note', the authors turn their attention to the tools of the art, the instruments and the singing voice. Here, too, nature plays a part, as for example in John F Deane's 'The Upright Piano', which tells of a failed attempt to row a piano by curragh across the sound to an island during heavy rainfall. When the instrument leans over and sinks down, it is as though it has taken its rightful position at last among the 'busy-fingered currents' that 'perform a suite / of intricate and burble-delicate water music', the melodious words matching the underwater music perfectly. Just stopping to listen to an aboriginal didjeridu will cause lyrebirds to nest 'in the devious loops / of your branching hair', Louis de Paor predicts in 'Didjeridu'; and again employing natural images Annie Deppe's poem 'The Throat Singers', about an Inuit song contest, describes how one of the singers 'lays down a challenge // with the sounds of muffled snow, / the other improvises riffs / like ice cracking.' The skin of Michael Longley's bodhran echoes 'All weathers that rattle / The windows, bang the door: / A storm contained, hailstones / Melting on its diaphragm.' The body, too, with all its natural inclinations has to have a hand in the proceedings. According to Peter Sirr's thoughtful introduction to 'Three Poems', 'the bodily experience of poetry is crucial', but this is even truer of music, not only for listeners but also and particularly for singers and players. The 'Singer' in Theo Dorgan's sequence is 'away somehow to where the song starts / and sure of every breath I will take from now.' Pete Mullineaux's piper fills the bellows with air and flies 'above the Walls of Limerick / the never ending Siege of Ennis'. In 'The Fado House of Argentina Santos', Mary Noonan hears a 'silver-haired fadista' in Lisbon singing 'in broken tremolo for the old dreams, for Lisboa // for what was lost'; and taking this a step further into the sphere of EU squabbles, Thomas McCarthy recalls in his playful 'Bel Canto' a Latvian mezzo-soprano's rendering of a Rossini aria 'with a restrained sweetness', as the strings rather reluctantly join in, not unlike countries joining the EU: 'It was Europe trying to adjust itself'.

While it is notoriously difficult to write about music, it seems that natural metaphors and images offer themselves freely to the writers to make us experience music almost as a form of physical assimilation. We are like the woman in Peter Fallon's poem 'Sean Nós' who couldn't hear, but once the singer placed her hand on his Adam's apple to feel the frequencies of the vocal chords vibrating in his throat, 'she felt and heard thoroughly'. The voice of Enda Wylie's charismatic 'Cúil Aodha Singer' 'moves strong and natural', Ciaran O'Driscoll echoes Ed Reavy's own words in his description of composing a fiddle tune, the music taking its form like 'an ice-cube moving on its meltwater'. Hugo Hamilton's concise excerpt from his novel 'Disguise' about a trumpet player and his favourite instrument condenses a 'life time of departures and comebacks' into a few lines, with the trumpet playing the role of companion, lover and working tool: '…the weight in his hands. The kiss of brass on his lips. He is known for swinging it over his shoulder like a shovel or a pitchfork…'

In the third chapter, 'A Sad Air's Best for Night', laments and elegies for musicians and singers, loved ones and friends are assembled: in 'Nine Years', Chris Agee movingly mourns his daughter who died as a small child. Eiléan Ní Chuilleanáin's 'Hofstetter's Serenade', an elegy for the poet's musician sister written 25 years after her much-too-early death, recalls Máire at eleven playing the famous serenade: 'the pure line of sound that grows, / rising dipping never landing on the same spot'. That line, like time, 'drew her along, the string and the bow, towards / the moment I saw her breath leaving her body and the silence began.' Silence and emptiness are the physical correlatives of the absence of life and of music. Rory Gallagher leaves an empty stage behind; so do the Miami Showband in Paul Durcan's lament for the members of the popular music group massacred by loyalist gunmen in Northern Ireland. If nature, as in Moya Cannon's poem 'Lament', can teach us the grammar of grief, of how to 'mark our losses with a cry', so can music train its melodies 'directly on the heart / when its resistance sinks, like temperatures, / to a day's end low: music that tells of how / things stand in the troubled world', as Dennis O'Driscoll says in 'Nocturne, Op. 2'. In the sonnet's last couplet the poet arrives at the insight that the fearful darkness of some music, 'a slow movement's stark conclusion', rings sadly true, a response which is echoed by Colm Tóibín's meditation on 'the dark truth lurking at the edge of things closer to history and knowledge and the great silence to come'. (Tóibín's longer article links music and visual art, inspired as it is by the work of the English artist Cornelia Parker.) Both Hugh Maxton in 'War and Music' and Eugene O'Connell in 'Blind Faith' touch upon another distressing topic: the cynical abuse of music by those in power. But there is consolation in nature amidst pain, illness and deep sorrow.

Macdara Woods, during a long spell in hospital, 'the salt fields by the sea', is cheered by hearing 'the loud dawn chorus / Another night has gone / Melted in the blue of the morning / And the great wide world spins on.' Leanne O'Sullivan's 'In Your Sleep', which is inspired by Vaughan Williams's The Lark Ascending, leaves it open whether the beloved will recover from a serious illness or not: 'Oh my dreamer, / are you a bird reviving in a summer field? / Was it the lark ascending that you heard', and Kathleen McCracken's elegy 'A Minor' compares the pain of loss to a 'long-drawn violet drawl / across the minor key of A', the key considered by some composers as most adequate for expressing sorrow. In 'Grief' by Geraldine Mitchell, 'grief // breaks / on the grace note / of a wren'. There are elegies for Elvis by Martina Evans and Leland Bardwell, for Seán Ó Riada and the piper Patsy Touhey, an eloquent elegiac poem in memory of the insane musical genius Adolf Wölfli by Ted Deppe, a bittersweet story by Ken Bruen about a woman who loved Johnny Cash, and Julie O'Callaghan's poem 'Saturday Afternoon in Dublin' describes a sorrowful time spent listening to Dietrich Fischer-Dieskau sing Gustav Mahler songs. Matthew Sweeney's poem 'Into the Air', in memory of Seamus Heaney, tells of the harpist found playing by the graveside in the dark, two days after the poet was buried, as if by invitation of the poet 'to set everything right.'

The fourth chapter is light-hearted and celebratory, but as the title 'Girl in a Wheelchair Dancing' suggests, this is not always easily won. Among other themes, youth is a central subject in this chapter. The girl in Mark Granier's poem is dancing so blissfully to U2 that she takes 'a new constellation, The Chariot' for a 'wild spin'. Pat Boran in 'Young Master' overhears a young kid practising the drums in the community centre 'below high barred windows' that let in 'bars of light' in which 'the dust motes swirl and bloom / as if something invisible had lifted them / and held them now, nebulous, but free.' The future life choices of the young drummer seem to lie between barred windows and freedom. They are as circumscribed as those of the more privileged public school boys singing in the chapel in James Harpur's 'Jubilate': 'we sing like lions, a pride of one / primeval roar – five hundred gentlemen // like chanting Millwall skinheads at the Den.' Leontia Flynn's 'By My Skin' is a witty tribute to a father with a great repertoire of songs which he performs while treating his small daughter's eczema, with 'a roll of cotton, / a soft-shoe routine, and a pound of soft white paraffin'. With richly evocative imagery, Emmanuel Jakpa celebrates the beauty of his African childhood landscape, story-telling and birdsong. Paula Meehan is visited by the ghosts of the long dead who come to her at night to foxtrot around her kitchen after she had played an old 78 record found under rubble in the granary, with the Bell Boys of Broadway performing 'Two-Buck Tim from Timbuctoo'. The poet wishes she could join their dance: 'step out onto their plane / spiral down a rain-washed road, let some ghostly partner / take the lead, become another migrant soul.' The nightingale in Medbh McGuckian's exquisitely mysterious poem 'Novena' sings 'on long light musky / evenings of a common blue stained with fabled / raindrops to a spangled veil.' The radio plays a prominent part in several poems in this chapter – its music programmes convey a sense of what John McAuliffe, after listening on long wave to RTÉ's The Long Note, a repeat from 30 years earlier, describes as 'continuity'. In Vona Groarke's 'Music from Home' we are told that even though the radio warns that the roads are nigh impassable, 'the tune, the first notes / of the opening year's slow air' will arrive nevertheless. And in Derek Mahon's 'Morning Radio', 'the merciful / Voice of Tom Crowe // Explains with sorrow / That the world we know / is coming to an end', but as the poet ironically informs us: 'The sun shines, / And a new day begins / To the strains of a horn concerto.'

Chapter five is the most personal of all the chapters, presenting a variety of memories and stories of music and musical encounters by the writers themselves. Not surprisingly, many are in the form of non-fiction prose. Michael Coady's memoir, for instance, 'Three Men Standing at the Met', which lends this chapter its title, is an eloquent and moving narrative of immigrants' lives in New York as much at the mercy of the forces of destiny as Donna Leonora or Don Alvaro in Verdi's opera. Three young penniless Irishmen, the poet's father and his brothers, visit the Metropolitan Opera in New York for the first time and fall under the spell of Verdi's music and the beautiful voice of Rosa Ponselli. The stories of their lives are told in a few paragraphs of concise and unsentimental prose. Dermot Bolger remembers Séamus Ennis, and it is appropriate that his poem is dedicated to another great musician, Tony MacMahon. Tom French pays poetic tribute to music-obsessed musician and singer friends and teachers, within the framework of his essay 'Like Cherry Flakes Falling', and Rachel McNicholl remembers her great-aunt, a courageous and fiercely independent organist and music teacher who 'conducted decades of choirs, / led thousands of hymns. / There was talk of naming a roundabout after her' – a sign that she had reached the summit of local fame and popularity. Joan McBreen hearing her daughter play the piano is assailed by troubled childhood memories, and in his poem 'Ship in the Night', Gerard Smyth relates how he 'was the boy who listened for hours / to broadcasts from a ship in the night', a lovely image of the vessel with a cargo of songs cruising up and down under the flag of music with no other assignment but to provide enjoyment for countless listeners. Iggy McGovern recalls the choral singing of 'pitch-challenged' choirboys, and in Peter Woods's spirited description of an all-night session the music was 'flowing together like liquid from different directions towards the one level.' Brian Leyden reminisces about the era of transistor radios and the 'pirate ship broadcasts from Radio Caroline and then fabulous 208: Radio Luxemburg'. Justin Quinn, who had never really paid much attention to songs, recounts the experience of memorising lullabies and folk tunes to sing to his babies at night while rocking them back to sleep, and increasingly becoming fascinated with the strangeness and beauty of their texts and melodies and their hypnotic rhythms. Two poems from a longer sequence about Michael Davitt entitled 'Land League Cottage' by Catherine Phil McCarthy describe how the lonely young wife finds consolation in music: 'I lifted the lid of my piano / to sound the worn ivory keys and sing – Love's Old Sweet Song'. There is an inventive and experimental prose piece by Rita Ann Higgins about driving to Connemara as a young girl with a father who lilted along the way while the daughter 'mimed' a lilt beside him. The piece packs a hard punch: the intimacy of the lilting comes at a price, and trying to retrieve a lost childhood and a lost language can be painful and in vain.

The writings in the final chapter, 'Listening to Bach', are dedicated to revered and illustrious musicians and composers, but they are more than just panegyrics. On the contrary, they read as though the writers had access to practice- and work-rooms; or examined manuscripts, score sheets, composition styles; or even shared isolated, sometimes rough lives on the road with them. Kerry Hardie perceptively honours the great Maya Homburger, who, while playing, vanishes behind the music, the most difficult art to accomplish: 'There's something in the presence, in the carriage, / a dignity that makes the player disappear, as though a lamp's been trimmed and lit and lifted'. Harry Clifton visits the contemporary Korean composer Song-On Cho in her Cologne apartment whose life and musical expression are haunted by her troubled past. Camille Saint-Saëns himself is given a voice in Caitríona O'Reilly's poem 'The Swan Theme', describing the moment of inspiration which took the composer by surprise: 'That the vision when it came, / should be of such a nature: / an interruption of swans. // Above the buffeting rhythm of their wings / I heard their voices singing to each other / and so the melody composed itself'. In the excerpt from Ciaran Carson's 'Last Night's Fun', the poet, himself a fine traditional musician, memorably tells of live recordings made in the early '70s of the great accordion player Joe Cooley. The resonance and beat of the language comes close to the soundtrack of a session in full swing: 'The plectral, gunky sound of the banjo is just right for the business in hand.[…], Joe drawing out the wild notes in places, making deft little chromatic runs in others – bits and bytes and phrases[…]. And the place is jumping: whoops and gulders, clicking bottles, tapping feet.' In Mary O'Malley's 'Footsteps', Seosamh Ó hÉanaí (Joe Heaney), the great traditional singer who left Connemara and went to 'plough the rocks of foreign cities / With unshed songs and my bare hands', remembers working as a navvy yet retaining his pride in his art and in his vocation as keeper of traditions.

The list of musicians and composers is long and varied: Gerard Hanberry pays tribute to Townes Van Zandt; Deirdre Cronin captures the exuberant spirit of Micho Russell's sessions in Doolin in her poem 'No Strings Attached'; Joseph Woods spends a summer listening to Chet Baker recordings; and Johnny Doran, Ronnie Drew, Phil Lynott and John McKenna are remembered. In his homage to Beethoven 'I Shall Hear in Heaven', Paddy Bushe, leaving his house at night for a walk while Beethoven is playing on the stereo, imagines himself a conductor bowing 'Ceremoniously to the orchestra of the stars'. The last two poems in this final chapter are dedicated to two great classical composers. In Sinéad Morrissey's 'Shostakovich', the composer, who after accusations of 'formalism' had fallen from grace in Stalin's Soviet Union, reflects on how he concealed messages underneath 'the top notes' of his compositions, where 'a strong strange melody pulsed', the frenzied 'theme of evil' as Shostakovich himself called it, recurring again and again in his work: 'the sound of a man's boots from behind the mountain', the frantic rhythm of the dictator dancing on the graves of his victims. In contrast to the despair and fury of Shostakovich's music, Pearse Hutchinson's wonderfully laconic 'Listening to Bach' leaves us cheered and hopeful that there's no real need to write about angels as long as we can listen to Bach. It seems that music has the last word after all.

We know that this *fermata* is a small pause within a much larger landscape of music honoured and acknowledged by the written word, and we regret that we could not include everyone who has written in the spirit of music. Bernard MacLaverty's *Grace Notes* is a work of profound insight into that spirit, as is Roddy Doyle's *The Commitments*. Neil Jordan's work carries music in its core; so does the poetry of Paul Muldoon. Tom Murphy's plays are like small symphonies; Edna O'Brien's words are like a tuning fork on ivory. And a new generation of writers is making its own mark and soundtrack in literature. We hope that our selection in *fermata* reminds readers of the work of these and other writers who illuminate music with their words, and also that this anthology will spur more writing from the pulse beat of song, of music; and the song-music of nature and the infinite world.

We are deeply grateful to the writers who contributed to this book; to Mícheál Ó Súilleabháin for his insightful foreword, Miriam de Búrca for her beautiful artwork, Christy McNamara for the memorable photographs. Our sincere and abiding gratitude goes to everyone who supported our *Fund it* campaign to publish this book – without your help *fermata* would not have seen the light. A special thanks to our publishers at Artisan House Connemara: Vincent Murphy, Creative Director, for his inspired design work and Mary Ruddy, Editorial Director; and above all we thank the musicians, singers, music makers and writers who enrich this world beyond measure.

Songbirds in the Stairwell

John **Montague**

Hearth Song

for Seamus Heaney

1

The Niall's cottage had one:
it lived under a large flagstone,
loving the warmth of the kitchen.

Chill or silent, for whole days,
it would, all of a sudden, start
its constant, compelling praise.

And all of us, dreaming or chatting
over the fire, would go quiet,
harkening to that insistent creak,

Accustoming ourselves all over again
to that old, but always strange, sound,
coming at us from under the ground,

Rising from beneath our feet,
welling up out of the earth,
a solitary, compulsive song

Compound for no one, a tune
dreamt up under a flat stone,
earth's fragile, atonal rhythm.

2

And did I once glimpse one?
I call up that empty farmhouse,
its blind, ghostly audience

And a boy's bare legs dangling
from a stool, as he peers
through a crack in the flagstones

And here it strikes up again,
that minute, manic cellist,
scraping the shape of itself,

Its shining blue-black back
and pulsing, tendril limbs
throbbing and trembling in darkness

a hearth song of happiness.

John **Montague**

Windharp

for Patrick Collins

The sounds of Ireland,
that restless whispering
you never get away
from, seeping out of
low bushes and grass,
heather-bells and fern,
wrinkling bog pools,
scraping tree branches,
light hunting cloud,
sound hounding sight,
a hand ceaselessly
combing and stroking
the landscape, till
the valley gleams
like the pile upon
a mountain pony's coat.

Michael **Longley**

The Stairwell

for Lucy McDiarmid

I have been thinking about the music for my funeral –
Liszt's transcription of that Schumann song, for instance,
'Dedication' – inwardness meets the poetry of excess –
When you lead me out of your apartment to demonstrate
In the Halloween-decorated lobby the perfect acoustic
Of the stairwell, and stand among pumpkins, cobwebby
Skulls, dancing skeletons, and blow kisses at the ceiling,
Whistling Great War numbers – 'Over there', 'It's a Long,
Long Way', 'Keep the Home Fires Burning' (the refrain) –
As though for my father who could also whistle them,
Trench memories, your eyes closed, your head tilted back,
Your cheeks filling up with air and melody and laughter.
I hold the banister. I touch your arm. Listen, Lucy,
There are songbirds circling high up in the stairwell.

Seamus **Heaney**

The Canopy

It was the month of May.
Trees in Harvard Yard
Were turning a young green.
There was whispering everywhere.

David Ward had installed
Voice-boxes in the branches,
Speakers wrapped in sacking
Looking like old wasps' nests

Or bat-fruit in the gloaming –
Shadow Adam's apples
That made sibilant ebb and flow,
Speech-gutterings, desultory

Hush and backwash and echo.
It was like a recording
Of antiphonal responses
In the congregation of leaves.

Or a wood that talked in its sleep.
Reeds on a riverbank
Going over and over their secret.
People were cocking their ears,

Gathering, quietening,
Stepping onto the grass,
Stopping and holding hands.
Earth was replaying its tapes,

Words being given new airs:
Dante's whispering wood –
The wood of the suicides –
Had been magicked to lover's lane.

If a twig had been broken off there
It would have curled itself like a finger
Around the fingers that broke it
And then refused to let go

As if it were mistletoe
Taking tightening hold.
Or so I thought as the fairy
Lights in the boughs came on.

Eamon **Grennan**

Untitled

Like sweet bells jangled in a minor key, starlings make in the big sycamore
Their autumnal music. Invisible from down here, their throats are open

To ripeness in the air, its *mellow fruitfulness* and that slight musky edge
Which may inflame them to this rhapsody of rapt cacophony, this annual tribal

Intoxication of the larynx that won't stop fattening, falling, improvising
One fleeting tune from their collective heart. Each year I hear this concert

That goes on for days, as if the whole congregation had taken leave of its
Sober senses, taken its note and cue from some soul hymnal – a dark choir

Of voices tuning, turning to flame, a harvest of bittersweet orchard chords
Saved from summer, pickled a little, offered up now while there's still time.

Vona **Groarke**

The Garden as Music and Silence

Only a roofline tin whistle
practising 'The Parting Glass'
construes the gap
between lupin and rose
as possible held breath.

Inside of which
it falls to me to imagine
the blue of cornflowers
has knowledge
of gothic windows
and tapestried plainsong.

Also, that Tuesday's red geraniums
might have something to say
about avowal

and the poppy seedheads
something about
presentiment

they learn
to keep
to themselves.

Chris **Agee**

The nightingales

and the stars
singing ensemble
one chill night
whose Spartan poem
I forgot
to write

Žrnovo, Croatia
2012-2013

Pearse **Hutchinson**

A Findrum Blackbird

Were there nightingales here before the Adze-head croziered?
and maybe she left us
alongwith the serpent?
How should a snake and a nightingale con*sort*?
She hardly wrenned it on his eagle-back,
unless he was Mexican – or did she guide him
Back to the garden of eden?

But never mind, we have the blackbird still –
de Ierse nachtegaal, as Johann Jacob van Eyck
might well have called him
peddling all over flanders unearthly flute-music –
what nightingale could ever sing
so well as that blind wanderer?

Perched acrest a lilac-bush
just inside the front gate
black-and-yellow music
turns a garden into a glade-scriptorium,
brings back those pagan monks,
and fills my deaf harmonious kitchen-window
with yellow-and-black music.

Thomas **Kinsella**

Song of the Night

Philadelphia

A compound bass roar
an ocean voice
Metropolis in the ear
soft-thundered among the towers below
breaking in a hiss of detail
but without wave-rhythm
without breath-rhythm
exhalation without cease
amplified
of terrible pressure
interrupted by brief blasts and nasal shouts
guttural diesels
a sky-train waning in a line of thunder.

I opened the great atlas on the desk.

The Atlantic curved on the world.

Carraroe

Our far boundary was Gorumna island
low on the water, dotted
with granite erratics, extended grey-green
along the opposite shore of the bay
toward the south Connemara series.

On our shore, among a tumble of boulders
on the minced coral, there was one
balanced with rugged edge upward,
stuck with limpets. Over it,
with the incoming tide, the waters

wash back and forth irregularly
and cover and uncover the brown angles.
Films of liquid light run
shimmering, cut by shell-points, over
stone inclines and clotted buds of anemones.

The films fatten with plasm and flow and fill
more loosely over the rock and gradually drown it.

Then larger movements invade from further out,
from the depths,
alive and in movement. At night-time

in the wind, at that place,
the water-wash lapped at itself under the rocks
and withdrew rustling down the invisible grains.
The ocean worked in dark masses in the bay
and applied long leverage at the shore

*

We were finished, and quiet.
The music was over.
The lamp hissed in the tent.

We collected the cooking things
and plates and mugs and cutlery
scattered around us in the grass,
everything bone cold,
and put it all in the plastic basin.

I unhooked the lamp and made my way down
flickering over the rocks with the children
to the edge of the ocean.

A cell of light hollowed around us
out of the night. Splashes and clear voices echoed
as the spoons and knives were dug down
and enamel plates scooped under water
into the sand, and scraped and rinsed.

I held the lamp out a little over the sea.
Silvery sand-eels seethed everywhere we stepped :
silvered and panicked through the shallows,
vanished – became sand – were discovered,
picked up with exclamations,
held out damp and deathly,
little whips fainted away
in wet small palms, in an iodine smell.

*

She was standing in a sheltered angle,
urgent and quiet,
'Look back…'
The great theatre of Connemara,

dark. A cloud bank stretched in folds
across the sky, luminous
with inner activity.

Centred on the beached lamp
a single cell of cold light,
part land and part living water,
blazed with child voices.

They splashed about the stark red basin,
pouncing. They lifted it and consulted.
Their crystalline laughter escaped upward,
their shadows huge.

We made off towards the rocky point
past the tent's walls flapping.

A new music came on the wind : string sounds hissing
mixed with a soft inner-ear roar
blown off the ocean; a persistent
tympanum double-beat (– 'darkly expressive,
coming from innermost depths…'). That old
body music. *Schattenhaft.* SONG OF THE NIGHT…
A long horn call, 'a single note
that lingers, changing colour as it fades …'

Overhead a curlew – God in Heaven ! –
responded!
'poignant …' Yes!
'hauntingly beautiful …' Yes!

The bay – every inlet – lifted
and glittered toward us in articulated light.
The land, a pitch-black stage
of boulder shapes and scalps of heaped weed,
inhaled.

A part of the mass
grated and tore, cranking harshly,
and detached and struggled upward
and beat past us along the rocks,
bat-black, heron-slow.

Mary **O'Malley**

Geography

Connemara has one language, two tongues.
It is knowing everyone's faults but your own.
It is never pulling together except in trouble
And then uniting.

It is not a brand name.
It is not a postcard
Nor a map. It is not a cottage, it is a house.
A small house
With its windows blocked in.
It is every word and footprint
Of the people that came from it.
It is not the million Euro cheque
The cement merchants bought it with.

It is Elephant John and the Pastime
And the streets of Cricklewood,
It is Graceland and cowboys,
Indians and guitars.
It is South Boston and East Berlin,
It is Shane McGowan's drunk tank
And a girl in a tile shop in Galway
Saying you have the fóidín meara.
It is being born faoi dhraíocht na farraige

It is not a private beach
It is a strand.
It is in South Boston and Levenshulme.
It is a state of mind and in the mind,
It lives and will stay alive
In the feet of its dancers,
In the mouths of its two-tongued poets,
In their broken language,
In the arms of its singers.

In the pure notes of its singers
It is held carefully as an ornament
Ó bhéal go béal
Ó áit go háit
Ó Shasana go Ros a' Mhíl
Ó Scaird ar maidin go Páras san oíche
Go mbeidh sé sínte choíche
Mar amhrán álainn san aer.

David Wheatley

Klangfarbenmelodie

Enter the haze

a lake by Humber orchestrated

for woodwind and strings (vole in the grass)

oboe and cello (water rail's shriek)

slant sun lighting the lake's

touch paper over its tidelines (smew in the reeds)

cloud of teeming harmonies filtered

through tympani and brass (diving grebe)

swelling double-bass scrape on the muddy bottom

lacustrine synaesthesia in the key

of bladder campion and hawthorn scrub

time signature blood-spill twilight red

Schoenberg's Third Orchestral Piece Op. 15

to the tune of 'I hate to see the evening sun go down...'

and the water seeping into your boots where you stand

and the song on each harebell's tongue

by puddle and lake and the umber impassable sea

asking only

carry me over

Kerry **Hardie**

Leaf-Fall

for Séan

'Chestnuts are the stubbornest.'
The pithy brown husks
that shielded the fruits
lie scattered about on the grass.
Also leaves.
But so many still on the trees.

'It takes a frost.
Don't you remember?'

Yes, he remembers.
The first bitter night
and the leaves all unhook.
They drift in the stillness,
they settle like moths on the grass.

He likes these hidden patterns and decisions:
trees, opening their hands in the night,
letting fall
what they have no more use for;
likes cycles, secrets, metaphysics.

'Sound,' he said
'is the least of music – '

And flourishes of trumpets
furiously blew,
their voices streaming
silently
onto the air.

Matthew **Sweeney**

The Canary

A canary in a cage sang to me
as I walked through the market.

I stopped. It sang louder,
so loud I thought its yellow body

would burst. I touched a bar
of the cage. The canary went quiet,

raised one foot and observed me,
then began singing again –

a much happier tune this time.
I knew I had to buy it, and

after a bit of haggling in Arabic,
of which I knew one word,

I emerged, holding the cage.
The canary sang an aria.

We were followed by feral cats.
Passers-by stared at me.

There was the problem of the plane –
how could I get that cage on?

The canary was tiny. If I dumped
the cage, it would fit in my pocket.

I could tie its beak shut, although
I wanted it to keep singing.

Anyway, I'd meditate in the hotel.
Then I'd know what to do.

Moya Cannon

Song in Windsor, Ontario

Ice whispers
as it crushes against
steelbound, staggering timbers
in the Detroit river.

Great plates of ice from the lakes
catch on the banks,
turn under the March sun,
crumple each other
to show
how mountain ranges are made.

And on the wooden pylons,
a small bird
is back with the seed of music,
two notes,
the interval of desire,
registered on the stirring cities.

Michael **O'Dea**

The Green Road

The blackthorns above Fanore
are flight rooted;
they are folklore's skeletons,
beggars of the green road.

Scoured to the knuckle,
stunted on Burren karst,
they are the hags on the mountain
hunched from Atlantic gales.

Yet even this stone-weary day,
with hunger perched on their throats,
a robin is singing in each
notes that singe the February air.

Beneath the huddling sky,
into the ear of the green road
it pours, clear as water,

Eva **Bourke**

Swallows

I can't believe they don't know what they are doing,
that delight is unknown to them as they gather
preparing for the long and terrible journey.
It cannot merely be all programme, hard-wire, protein,
plasma, synapse, cellular. They are too expert
at elevation and elation, those twin joys.
The other day I walked down a street
of small grey houses in my neighbourhood
and saw them take off and settle around a pole
from which five parallel wires were strung
to other poles, from those onto the eaves. There was
such excitement in the air, flutter
and twitter of a great activity, swing-up, dip
and vibrato of landing on the shakiest of landing strips
their arrow-tailed dark bodies arranged on the
electric wires like quavers on a large grey sheet of music.
I picked out and sang the melody they'd composed:
in thirds and fifths: two Ds, two Gs, two Bs, and two more Ds
then the whole gamut upped and modulated in one lift-off
to the top line F and with extravagant slurs
and glissandi flocked onto a nearby gutter.
A neighbour opening her door behind me said
they're gathering to say goodbye and will soon be away.
I sang the swallows' song to her as best I could
but never mastered the mordents of farewell
as they slipped past us and beyond.

Alice **Lyons**

marram

a word
we love

marram
silverpoint on dune

in midden-rich Shelly valley

we yell

marram!

ampersand!

gossamer!

words are jellies
our mouths warm

words are ice floes
melting steadily

we go out on them anyhow

isn't *weird* a weird word
when you really think about it?

In high sun
marram casts
scythes
such cuts

you

are falling

in half-moons

dune ladder

daughter

fringe-sickle
snagging
mascared lashes

I adjust
only mentally

red dots droppered
black nail varnish

wings of moths
we minute-trapped
last May
on Inishmurray

marram
sea mirror

mar haulm
grace grass

marram
early word

ever

binding
loose sands

with tough rhizomes

Joseph **Woods**

Singing Gate

from Ballyowen (a sonnet sequence)

A clutch of cars driving to the mouth
of the valley for a hike up to the heavens
when the heavens opened down on us.
Declining to get drenched as you
and the others headed off in the downpour,
I dithered then dipped into Bowen's Court,
somewhere in the 1840s in a car assailed,
buffeted by wind and rain.
The land outside washed desolate as the event
I travelled through in a stranded car.
Soaked, you poured back with a story of how
you heard music in the wet wilderness below.
Its source the high bar of a gate you crossed,
rain-rusted sound-holes and the wind wildly playing them.

Peter **Fallon**

Home from Home

He was skimming stones
across the ice of Broughton Pond.
The further they skated
the louder they broadcast
from that beyond
song that was birdsong
sounding on and on.

Maurice **Riordan**

Faun Whistling to a Blackbird

This afternoon a blackbird came to my nook
while I was sleeping off a feed of goat curds
and Retsina. I'd rented one of those dreams
from Morpheus in which I was roughing it
with A down the Glens – or was it her cousin X?
The bird startled me as she foraged near my kit,
amongst the mosses where notepad and pen
had slipped from my hand. Maybe she mistook
the pad for bread since the pages were white
with some crumbs about growing old and sex?
She took flight, but only as far as the eglantine
behind my head. I tootled to her, *Sweet bird,*
why abuse a poet lost amid his fuzzy dreams…
She whistled back, some Goidelic curse she'd heard
beside the Erne or Belfast Lough. Such a flyting
we had, such a duel or duet we struck up then
as our brains fired, two heated creatures reared
in muck and wind becoming soul-companions
under the Sicilian sun – her feathered, me furred.

Dermot **Healy**

The Litany of the Wagtail

Chirp of the flirt,
scurry through the blur,
sudden snatch of song.

Pulse gatherer.
Time keeper.

Sidestep of the polka,
tig on the street,
marionette of the wind.

Altar-boy's curtsy,
white thread of tweed.

Ceaseless diving-rod.

Warrior of the mirror.
Noon trill.
The cry from beyond the sickbed.

Groom of sweet wooing,
morning tuning-fork,
skiff of the field.

Breast of the hailstone.
Nib dipped in clear ink.

Strike of the dandelion clock,
bounce of brightness,
chase down-the-wind.

Rosary of shingle,
loyal chime of winter,
quill of the rain-bead.

Welcome eye on the sea-wall,
slim reed of willow,
bib of black silk.

Sheath of wings,
needle of the spinning compass,
fast dart past the cold horse.

Rain baton.
Cry above the gunshot of the sea.

Joyful alarm beyond the gable,
companion of the short day.

Quick skip of the heart,
glad bell at storm's end.

Gabriel **Rosenstock**

Ekphrastic haiku

Young Gypsy Musician

some roads go on
with no end in sight . . .
gypsy boy

伸びる道
果てなど見えず
ジプシー少年

tá bóithre ann
is níl aon deireadh leo . . .
garsún giofógach

sum rods gae on
wi nae end in sicht . . .
tinker laddie

Haiku translations
Japanese: **Mariko Sumikura**
Irish: **Gabriel Rosenstock**
Scots: **John McDonald**

Photography: **Eva Besnyö**

The Given Note

The Given Note

On the most westerly Blasket
In a dry-stone hut
He got his air out of the night.

Strange noises were heard
By others who followed, bits of a tune
Coming in on loud weather

Though nothing like melody.
He blamed their fingers and ear
As unpractised, their fiddling easy

For he had gone alone into the island
And brought back the whole thing.
The house throbbed like his full violin.

So whether he calls it spirit music
Or not, I don't care. He took it
Out of wind off mid-Atlantic.

Still he maintains, from nowhere.
It comes off the bow gravely,
Rephrases itself into the air.

John F **Deane**

The Upright Piano

That summer the heavens opened;
days you'd think
Noah come again, eels
squirming in the street and brown-water streams

harrowing the tarmac edges; birds
skimmed over the grasses, swallow, house-martin, swift;
starling flocks,
gossip-mongering in branches of the ash

lifted suddenly as one, though fractured,
sentence.
The coming by the house
of yet another down-pouring of rain

sounded at first like the titter-tattering
legs of rats
racing across the stretched-taut skins
of tympani.

When they hoisted down an old upright piano
off the pier's edge onto a curragh
and rowed carefully out across the sound towards the island,
the rains came harder,

blotting out the world;
the boat lurched sideways into the reaching arms of a wave; piano
leaned lazily over and sank and now –
under the rough-cast gurgling cacophonies, the gripe-words

of the flowing past of waters – you will hear
the busy-fingered currents
perform a suite
of intricate and burble-delicate water-music.

Mark **Granier**

Vulture Bone Flute

38,000 BC

Fitting to see the oldest airs
salvaged from a raptor – the air
of its wing – and there is music

in our bodies, drums and strings,
wind instruments fulfilling themselves
so blood and sweat sings

to surfaces, half-blinding those eyes
lost in the swing of a scythe,
a notched sword, the haulage

of hominid arms through foliage –
music that runs like sap
back to the root

of our species jogging on the spot
wired to an iPhone – chants, field hollers,
deafening wars, silences – the body

bearing the mind away
with riffs, keys, tones, variations
on what's in us and what will come

to blow through our bones.

Vona **Groarke**

Interval

Between acts, mindful
of the present tense
but beholden to what
has already occurred
or what might be going to

as a noun between two verbs
comes to marrow them both
until there is still enough
for the next thing to happen
and be happening again

in the way the opening note
of the second half
has the last note by heart
but doesn't either recall or predict
what plays out over time.

Better to aspire
to knowing as much
of what's done and
what remains to be done
as the pure note on the violin

knows about purfling
or applause, or about
the mastodon tusk
or Mongolian mare's tail
that goes into making the bow.

Eamon **Grennan**

Kate Singing

Her Junior High School graduation:
she's singing alone
in front of the lot of us –

her voice soprano,
surprising, almost
a woman's. The *Our Father*

in French, the new language
making her strange, out there,
full-fledged and

ready for anything. Sitting
together – her mother, her
father – we can hear

the racket of traffic
shake the main streets
of Jersey City as she sings

deliver us from evil,
and I wonder can she see me
in the dark here, years

from belief, on the edge
of tears. Doesn't matter. She
doesn't miss a beat, stays

in time, in tune – while into
our common silence I whisper
Sing, love, sing your heart out!

Matthew **Sweeney**

Do Wah Diddy Diddy Do

Singing *Do Wah Diddy Diddy Do*
I jumped off the white shaky bridge
into the River Lee, and swam back-
stroke towards town, past the closed-
down fancy hotel, with the red walls
of the old asylum looming up above
on the opposite bank, and a heron
eyed me from where he stood on one
leg in the shallow water – he clearly
didn't like my song so I sang louder
till he rose and flew away, circling
over me as if he couldn't believe me.

Do Wah Diddy Diddy Do I roared
at a kayak that passed me, earning me
a German expletive I replied to in
kind, barely disturbing the song's
rhythm then I veered left as the river
split, preferring to swim in the shade,
wishing I'd brought along a banana
tucked in my soggy pocket – the peel
would have floated and fed some gulls
and they would have liked my song,
then I climbed out, dripping, at the
Opera House, and I stopped singing.

Louis de Paor

Didjeridu

Ní mheallfaidh an ceol seo
nathair nimhe aníos
as íochtar ciseáin do bhoilg
le brothall seanma
na mbruthfhonn teochreasach.

Ní chuirfidh sé do chois cheannairceach
ag steiprince ar leac
gan buíochas ded aigne cheartaiseach
le spreang tais na gcasphort ceathach.

Má sheasann tú gan chor
ar feadh soicind amháin
nó míle bliain,
cuirfidh sé ealta liréan
ag neadú i measc na gcuach
id chlaonfholt cam,
                gorma
pearóidí   glasa
                dearga
ar do ghuaillí loiscthe
is cucabora niogóideach
ag fonóid féd chosa geala.

Beidh treibheanna ársa an aeir
ag cleitearnach timpeall ort,
ag labhairt leat i mbéalrá
ná tuigeann do chroí
gallghaelach bán.

Má sheasann tú
dhá chéad bliain ag éisteacht,
closifir ceolstair a chine
ag sileadh as ionathar pollta,
géarghoba éan
ag cnagadh plaosc,
ag snapadh mionchnámh,
agus doirne geala
ár sinsear cneasta
ag bualadh chraiceann na talún
mar a bheadh bodhrán
ná mothaíonn
                                        faic.

Louis **de Paor**

Didjeridu

This music is not played
to lure a snake
from the woven basket
of your distended belly
with a heat-wave of torrid notes
and swooning melodies.

It won't set your rebel foot
tapping on stone
to taunt your straitjacketed intellect
with squalls of hornpipes
and twisting slides.

If you stand
and listen, for a second
or a thousand years,
lyrebirds will nest
in the devious loops
of your branching hair,
green
blue parrots
red
will perch on your scalded shoulders
and a sarcastic kookaburra
make fun of your scorched white feet.
You'll hear parakeets and lorikeets
flutter round your head,
ancient tribes of the air
speaking a language
your wild colonial heart
cannot comprehend.

If you can stand
for a minute
or two hundred years,
you'll hear the songs
of his people bleed
from a punctured lung,
sharp beaks
pecking skulls,
snapping small bones,
while the bright fists
of our gentle ancestors
beat the skin of the earth,
like a bodhrán
that feels
nothing.

Annie **Deppe**

The Throat Singers

With a half hour left before closing
and most of the museum still unexplored,
why was I unable to leave

the exhibit on Inuit throat singers?
I kept pushing the button
that played a film of two old women –

are they sisters? – standing nose-to-nose
in what looks like a musical duel.
As one lays down a challenge

with the sounds of muffled snow,
the other improvises riffs like ice
cracking. How deep their voices are,

probing a place far lower than expected.
It's as if by descending
they can sing from the inside of things.

They sing the metal rod used to chip through ice.
They sing water welling up through the hole.
They sing the wind, the sled, the dogs.

And from somewhere at the back of their throats,
known from a time before their births, they sing fire
to guide the hunters safely home.

Each woman holds the other's gaze. Shoulders
rise and fall together, as they play
a game where everything in their world's at stake.

Now at night, after watching that film so many times,
I seem to hear, right on the edge of my understanding,
the singing of old women

dressed in the flowered clothes of schoolgirls.
I think they're singing the silver fish scooped
from a hole, as well as the crackling plastic bag

they use to carry those fish. They name
the tilt of telephone poles and the sound
of grass pushing up through snow,

and the wind, also, swirling through that grass.
I'm going to sleep to the snowmobile's whine,
to the rattle of the prefab home's aluminium door

and the electric can opener's miracle drone.
My prayers hum as the women sing to young girls
who've come to learn their song.

They weave in the girls' names –
Winnie and Sarah. Somehow I'm hearing
the names of my children, too.

Their voices hold the stars of an Arctic sky.
The aurora borealis
on a baby's cap. They hold the baby itself

as it's tucked into fold after fold of sleep.
I give myself to the sounds of voices
singing from the insides of things.

She's Easy

They're my things, she says,
washing the front step
until it sings
and cleaning the toilet.
She loved that programme
about the OCD'ers;
She felt closer to the cleaners
than the counters
or the checkers.
She was a clean fiend once
but she narrowed it down to
front step and toilet.
After that the house could fall down
for all she cared.
When she cleaned she sang,
mostly happy songs.
Elvis and Roy Orbinson,
Pretty woman walkin' down the street ...
She'd belt out
I found my thrill on Blueberry Hill.
The new water charges bother her though,
when she thought of the water charges
she couldn't sing.
The room in her head with the tunes
was locked down like Alcatraz.
She says she can't afford to pay
the water charges, simple as that.
I like a bath did I tell you that?
Yeah, I like a bath and a shower
just before and after I use the toilet.
Apart from that, I'm easy.

Peter **Fallon**

Sean Nós

Far in the west in a dark hotel
a singer was singing
a new song in an old style.

And a woman was listening
who couldn't hear.
She hadn't heard since she

was a girl. But, oh, she remembered
music; music she loved.
'Come here,' said the singer,

'come here to me now,'
and on his Adam's apple
he settled her hand

and he resumed his melody.
As the bits of an air
stirred into shape

she felt and heard thoroughly.

Theo **Dorgan**

Singer
#6

The pub door bangs shut, somebody calls for hush,
the singer begins. My head's an open cave
and back in the dark the song takes root, shadows
writhe and twist and push

towards starlight, rise and fall back, called out, fearful,
near, from time out of mind. Sung, the song is old
but by this made new, all of us rapt and quiet,
some of us tearful.

There by the fire, she must have just come in, coat
flecked with rain, a fine mist in her hair. She turns,
unhoods her grey eyes, looks through the song at me.
Time dies in my throat,

I am away somehow to where the song starts
and sure of every breath I will take from now.
Making an arrow of hands I part the crowd,
drawn by her dark art.

Singer
#62

Three days and nights I worked in a frenzy, paced
and stood frozen, chasing the tune, the phrases,
the notes and chords. The hardest was to find words
of adequate grace

and weight. I saw I had learned my craft but not
how to trust myself on the long plunge into
chaos, what can be found there, named and brought back.
That was a hard-fought

war – I wept, sweated, swore, built and tore back down
version and version, but I did it, I made
her song, gave up my name. It keeps itself, it
stands on common ground.

In the long years after, I would hear it played,
sung, in so many voices I could forget
the cost, hope she might somehow hear, accept it
as debt fully paid.

Gerard **Hanberry**

Lilter

No instrument ever mastered
not even the penny whistle.

Where would he have found time
for such 'nonsense' as a lad?

The barrow, the spade, splitting stones
with a loose-handled sledge.

Bits of tunes tipped in a ramshackle henhouse
tucked behind the shadow-gable of his mind.

The boat to England. Lurking, pint in hand,
on the edge of a Saturday night 'session'

or listening, ear tilted,
to a balladeer or fiddler,

through the drink-drenched wistfulness
of late night lock-ins.

Silent, until that wet day at tea-break in the site hut,
the gangerman absent,

he lilted a tune for the lads from home
ranged about on planks and cement bags,

a note-perfect jig skittering off his tongue,
surprising all, including himself.

They danced in their overalls and lead-heavy boots,
yelping and linking elbows, rising bomb-clouds of dry cement,

and he on an upturned bucket, lilting and clapping,
his hunched shoulders bouncing in time

until stifled at last by the swirling dust and the laughter
he made for the door

spread his new wings,
cock-crowed and was free.

Ciaran **O'Driscoll**

Catch

(Ed Reavy speaks)

It is good for poets to take their notebooks
to bed with them, for musicians to sleep
within an arm's reach of their instruments.
Not in vain have I been granted this talent,
a lantern of the mind that wakes me up.

This morning when my son called in to ask
about his roster in my plumbing business,
I told him that the first thing he must do
was listen to the tune I caught last night.
I played it and the boy approved my reel.

A gift of nature, night and urgency:
to slip from beside my dear one and go,
briskly as a fox, to the music-place,
my den of soundproof comfort, knowing well
the dear one just arrived won't wait around.

Last night I sat to play not knowing what
I'd make of the small tumult in my head
finding and losing form. But when I set
the bow to string, the tune took off alone,
an ice-cube moving on its meltwater.

Pibroch

for Robert Somerset

Boarding the coffin-ship for Canada,
paying their pittance to the foreign owners,
the clansmen found their piper lacked even that.
They could not face the far sea without music,
for the new land, that strange planet,
they needed the music of their own lost land.

So they begged the masters to let the piper
play his passage. But the masters of money
turned the pauper away,
money as always having no mercy on music,
except the music of its own blind, gaping wound.

So the people in their need scraped around in their poverty
and mustered the pittance for the music to travel,
and so the masters made a little more money,
but the festering hold was dancing,
lamentations swabbed the landless deck,
the creaking, rotting boat was outraged and blest.

Mary O'Malley

Footsteps

Christ, a man is doffed from cradle to grave.
First it was my own steps
Behind me on the Carna road
Coming late from a dance.

Thrown out of college for a cigarette
I met my father's coffin on the way home,
Sunday shoes on the gravelly path.
I quickstepped back to Dublin.

Before the bog could suck me in
Or the sea swallow me I went
To plough the rocks of foreign cities
With unshed songs and my bare hands,

My cardboard suitcase
Tied with string, an address in Southampton
On the back of a cigarette pack:
'Flow gently, sweet Afton, among the green braes...'

Look. I am the custodian of our songs.
I know the highest note permitted,
the longest line, the way the voice
Should settle in the throat.

Maybe Glasgow was a mistake. I left
With children pounding in my head and a wife.
Christ. I crossed the Atlantic and never looked back.
When you sing all else is silenced.

America, where the past ends six inches below
The asphalt. For years I left it all behind.
Then I heard them in New York, the old men
My teachers, shuffling on forty-second street.

Footsteps. They gather in the dark and swell
Like applause. Soon I will close my ears to all
But the little silver heel taps that have rung
Around my head like tuning forks

In the long silence, the pause before the living join
The slow processional circling of the dead.

Fleadh

for Brian O'Donnell

Fiddle

Stained with blood from a hare,
Then polished with beeswax
It suggests the vibrations
Of diaphanous wings
Or – bow, elbow dancing –
Follows the melted spoors
Where fast heels have spun
Dewdrops in catherine-wheels.

Flute

Its ebony and silver
Mirror a living room
Where disembodied fingers
Betray to the darkness
Crevices, every knothole –
Hearth and chimney-corner
For breezes igniting
The last stick of winter.

Bodhrán

We have eaten the goat:
Now his discarded horns
From some farflung midden
Call to his skin, and echo
All weathers that rattle
The windows, bang the door:
A storm contained, hailstones
Melting on this diaphragm.

Whistle

Cupped hands unfolding
A flutter of small wings
And fingers a diamond
Would be too heavy for,
Like ice that snares the feet
Of such dawn choruses
And prevents the robin
Ripening on its branch.

Pipes

One stood for the fireside
And the field, for windbag
And udder: milk and rain
Singing into a bucket
At the same angle: cries
Of waterbirds homing
Ripples and undertow –
The chanter, the drones.

Bel Canto

for Catherine Coakley

The year has been detained because of something offstage,
Some disturbance in the wings that had drawn the stage manager
And all his gruff attendants into a minor skirmish –
What might have seemed to the innocent as a skittish wind
Making the curtains flutter was in fact a delicate elbow
And a Greek or Cypriot raised knee coming to blows. The Irish
Need to remain in their seats, was what Ms. Lagarde said
As she came front-stage, checking her *Louis Vuitton* buttons,
Adjusting her coiffure. At least we were sitting here, my father
Said, so we can't be blamed for this wounded orchestra.
O patria! Dolce, e ingrate patria, the young Latvian beauty
Now sang with a restrained sweetness. Violins assembled
Doubtfully around her, but they all tried honestly to come in.
It was Europe trying to adjust itself, but more simply now:
It was Christine Lagarde and Elina Garanca together,
Making all the violins murmur, just murmur. There now,
My father whispered, that's it: *Tancredi*, Act 1, the *Andante*.

Derek **Mahon**

The Andean Flute

He dances to that music in the wood
As if history were no more than a dream.
Who said the banished gods were gone for good?

The furious rhythm creates a manic mood,
Piercing the twilight like a mountain stream.
He dances to that music in the wood.

We might have put on Bach or Buxtehude,
But a chance impulse chose the primal scream.
Who said the banished gods were gone for good?

An Inca frenzy fires his northern blood.
His child-heart picking up the tribal beam,
He dances to that music in the wood.

A puff of snow bursts where the birches brood;
Along the lane the earliest snowdrops gleam.
Who said the banished gods were gone for good?

It is the ancient cry for warmth and food
That moves him. Acting out an ancient theme,
He dances to that music in the wood.
Who said the banished gods were gone for good?

Mary **Noonan**

The Fado House of Argentina Santos

The women here are of a certain age
          their doubles hang in black and white
on the walls – photos showing
          the wailing women of 1930s Lisbon
hair set in bird's nests, eyebrows
          pencilled.

The ancient doyenne, queen of the *fadistas*
          sits in her lair by the door
a hawk in navy blue.
          From a serving-hatch framed in *azulejo*
her elder sister peers. Faithful retainer
          in black and *broderie anglaise*

her task is to fix lace doilies
          in bread baskets. And spy. Not a word
passes between her and the others –
          middle-aged *meninas* spilling
from worn needlepoint bibs, pinned in
          by tight bows at the waist. Nightly

                    they dance

their angry fandango on fallen arches and varicose veins
          battling, in the time between *fados*,
to get tubs of *bacalhau* down to the trestles
          where the drunken tourists wait.

On the half-hour, lights are flicked off,
          a silver-haired *fadista* steps from the shadows.
Cradling herself in a fringed shawl,
          she opens her throat and ululates
in broken tremolo for the old dreams, for Lisboa

                    for what was lost.

And her frilled serving-sisters stomp
          the dough-white flesh of their calves
and scowl.
          And Argentina Santos watches from the door.

Pearse **Hutchinson**

The Miracle of Bread and Fiddles

We were so hungry
we turned bark into bread.

But still we were hungry,
so we turned clogs into fiddles.

James **Joyce**

Lean out of the window

Lean out of the window,
Goldenhair,
I heard you singing
A merry air.

My book is closed;
I read no more,
Watching the fire dance
On the floor.

I have left my book,
I have left my room,
For I heard you singing
Through the gloom,

Singing and singing
A merry air.
Lean out of the window,
Goldenhair.

James **Joyce**

Tar go dtí an fhuinneog

Tar go dtí an fhuinneog
    'Niamh Chinn Óir.
Chuala tú 'canadh
    I do bhinnghlór.

Dhúnas an leabhar.
    Ní léim níos mó.
Breathnaím ar lasracha
    Ó óró.

D'fhágas an leabhar.
    Is an seomra d'fhág
Mar chuala mé amhrán
    Tríd an scáil.

Ag canadh os ard
    I do bhinnghlór.
Tar go dtí an fhuinneog
'Niamh Chinn Óir.

trans. Gabriel Rosenstock

Peter Sirr

Three Poems

Introduction

The cliché is that all poetry aspires to the condition of music. I think of Basil Bunting: Poetry, like music, is to be heard. It deals in sound – long sounds and short sounds, heavy beats and light beats, the tone relations of vowels, the relations of consonants to one another which are like instrumental colour in music.'

(Basil Bunting, *Strong Words*, eds W.H. Herbert and Matthew Hollis, Bloodaxe, 2000 p80)

He certainly applied this to his own work. Just look at the opening lines of 'Briggflatts' as music:

Brag, sweet tenor bull,
descant on Rawthey's madrigal,
each pebble its part
for the fells' late spring.
Dance tiptoe, bull,
black against May.
Ridiculous and lovely
chase hurdling shadows
morning into noon.
May on the bull's hide
and through the dale
furrows fill with May,
paving the slowworm's way.

You just want to stand back and listen to the noise this makes, relishing the river Rawthey's pebble-madrigal, the 'Ridiculous and lovely' image of the bull dancing. To write poetry is, or should be, an attempt to create a distinctive music, a tune of one's own. I do think the bodily experience of poetry is crucial. Charles Wright once said that poems should come out of the body 'like webbing from the spider.'

Maybe this is one of the reasons I'm attracted to music, why I find it hard to get through the day without at least a partial immersion in it. I hope some of it might rub off on me; I hope something of its power might be enticed into whatever writing I am at. Or I hope for some direct inspiration – of which more later. Only rarely have I attempted to write about music or in response to a particular piece, but two of the poems here are just that. 'Listening to Bulgarian Music' re-tells the story behind one of the tunes I was listening to on a now long lost tape: a contest between lovers and an unexpected victory.

'Music for Viols' was written after repeated listening to 'Good Againe' by the composer for viol, Tobias Hume. In that case some of the back story entered the poem: his irritation at the lute and lutenists. Who did they think they were, Dowland and the rest – did they imagine no one else could make music, did they really think the viol was a lesser instrument than the lute?

Still, I suppose he was entitled to his grumpiness. His music, which in fact owes more to the lute than he might pretend, is original and beautiful, which is why Captain Tobias Hume, whom it didn't seem to comfort or appease in any way, even in old age, will be remembered. The poem in its way tries to honour him and his music and the effect of hearing it played by the incomparable Jordi Savall.

My final offering is more definitely intertwined with music. It's one of a series of poems which are versions of originals by the Troubadour poets, poems written in Old Occitan between the twelfth and fourteenth centuries. Many of these were sung, and the music for some has survived. Listening to the music became the primary engine of translation: I gathered multiple versions of songs and let them soak in. One that I returned to obsessively was *Can vei la lauzeta* by Bernart de Ventadorn. It's probably impossible to reproduce the musical effect of the poem in English so my version is necessarily a rough copy. For the full effect you need the original, a decent dictionary and a few hours to listen to renditions by Paul Hillier, Gérard Zucchetto, Millenarium, Els Trobadors …

Listening to Bulgarian Music

God grant me crooked corn and a cool day
she prayed, and it happened.
At the end, his family conceded defeat
and trudged home, lit by their own gold.

The field was all hers and she moved
down the outnumbering sheaves
to where he stood, his body bent
above the stubble, waiting for her.

Music for Viols

Tobias Hume's *Good Againe*

Good again
this night, this late
to hear that tune and fall
again, the slow dark drag,
texture
of thickly branched trees
swaying above water,
of sound moving
from the farthest pit
to pour down.
God and the devil
must play the viol.
The door of the world
swings open
on Hume's excited figure.
After sadness, hunger,
royal blindness
to the great shame of this land
and those that do not help me
after a bellyful of snails
and the sniping of lutenists
good again to stand
with the night
in Jordi's hands
and listen
and walk in
as far as the tune will go.

Bernart de Ventadorn

The Lark

When I see the lark
beat his wings against the sun
self-forgetting, falling
for the sweetness of it
then such envy comes on me
of all who go rejoicing.
How is it my heart
is not crushed by desire?

So much I thought I knew
of love, who know nothing of it
who can't help loving
her from whom I'll have nothing.
All of my heart she has, all of me.
Her own self she has, all the world.
When she left, nothing stayed
but longing, nothing but love of her.

No power I've had, or control
from the instant
she let me look into her eyes,
the mirror that so pleased me.
Since I saw myself there
I've acted the fool,
as lost in its regard
as Narcissus at his pool.

I've done with that, I'll trust
no love again.
As once I defended them
now I'll leave women alone.
I am the fool on the bridge
befuddled by stone, landing in water,
I am the lark
that soared too high.

Since she gets no pleasure from my prayers
she can have no mercy:
there's nothing left but exile.
When I see the lark
I'll go away, somewhere under the sun:
I shall renounce song, I shall
rail against it, and hide
from love, and hide from joy.

trans. Peter Sirr

Pat **Boran**

Concert off Kensington High Street

By ten o'clock the site was alive:
Casey, the foreman, already chewing on his pencil,
a kettle boiled for the first strong teas,
and Cookey on the mixer had prepared
a wonderful cement that made the men's mouths water.

High up in the scaffolding
Big Bill sang the blues,
balanced delicately on an old black bucket
that doubled as a piano stool.

By noon he had finished the wall,
tinkling the ivory bricks into place
with so passionate a history of Basin Street
that Casey made a collection among the crowd
in a riddle, directing latecomers from the street
with his No Parking megaphone
to the less desirable, cement-bag seats.

Jan **Wagner**

giovanni gnocchi plays the cello

giovanni gnocchi is playing bach, while outside
there's the city, the summer, the heat.
but the most celestial bumblebee is here,
astray in the cool hall, flying lazily
from page to page, from note to note.

giovanni gnocchi is playing bach, but bach
is also playing him, making his fingers climb aloft
like pale sailors in the rigging,
while outside there's the heat, july, the city.
and everything hoists sail. and everything casts off.

trans. Eva Bourke

Hugo **Hamilton**

excerpt from ***Disguise***

A few days before his birthday, Gregor walked in the door and Daniel could not wait to tell him what was on his mind.
'Mama has got you a trumpet', Daniel said right away, before Gregor had even taken his jacket off.
'Wait,' Gregor said. 'Was that meant to be a secret?'
'Yes', Daniel answered with eyes wide open. 'It's your birthday present,' he said.

Gregor may have had a hint even before that, because he once mentioned the notion of buying the trumpet his friend had lent to him, but Mara discouraged that, saying they would start saving up for the best. Nonetheless, it was still a surprise when they celebrated with a cake and candles and table cloth on the table and Mara dressed up. He unwrapped the gift pretending he knew nothing, carefully taking off the paper, embracing her with such life in his eyes. He could work out how long she had been saving up and how hard it was not to say a word.

How often has he played it all over the world, in so many bars and jazz clubs, never once forgetting that moment when she gave it to him, sometimes thinking about it all evening and then putting it out of his head so as not to allow the feeling to get the better of him. Countless bulging notes have been blown through that piece of brass. It has lost its gloss, but it still releases an exceptional musical scream in his hands. The horn has become dented by collisions along the way, but it has character like no other trumpet. A sweetness, a clarity, a pure, lived-in sound that only a well-played trumpet can have and that only fellow trumpet players can really appreciate. He's been offered money for that instrument by well-known players. Enough to buy himself a new suite of instruments. In fact he has bought other trumpets since then, for their own particular tone, but none of them play quite like this one. None of them have that much biography in them.

He has often spoken about the weight of it in his hands. The kiss of brass on his lips. He is known for swinging it over his shoulder like a shovel or a pitchfork in a momentary pause at concerts, a style that other musicians have since copied. He was born for that instrument, Mara always said whenever she heard him rip another deep, declamatory note into their small apartment, a note that probably shook the whole block into life, like the sound of a cow lowing in the courtyard. The neighbours must have said:
'Oh no. Somebody's bought a shagging trumpet.'

He still plays some of the clubs in Berlin when he's asked to join a reunion gig. He likes the relaxed companionship of musicians playing their stuff together and hardly speaking to each other. His big brass larynx. The unmistakable warm, half-drunk, country-wedding sound of the trumpet. A fat, laconic, outdoor echo. The whole inner road movie feeling that comes out of every time he lifts the instrument up to his lips. He jokes about making a big comeback, but he's really much happier doing his own thing now, playing for fun, instead of for a living, listening to younger players, teaching and watching his own trademark licks passing on to another generation. He's had too many comebacks already. An entire lifetime of departures and comebacks.

Gerard **Smyth**

Little Mysteries

for Philip King

After a few false starts, the harmonica player
picks up a bluesy melody or slow air,
a cracked tune or one that was lost
and found, borrowed and returned
but never a burden to the one who carries it.
Maybe *Bless the Weather* or *Sweet Little Mystery*
or something more traditional
from a place that never runs out of rhythms
in the hills of Clare or Mississippi.

And blessed are the song-makers –
first the forgotten ones who sing no more
and now the troubadours of a new century chorus.
Theirs are the melodies that wander the earth,
from festival to festival
in those gardens where thousands pitch their tents

or that bit of a tune left in the air
when bow and fiddle are laid to rest
and the singer sits down,
his mouth dried up
like the red rose of blood on Connolly's shirt.

Enda **Wyley**

Cúil Aodha Singer

for Iarla

You are different
when you sing the aching notes
your fathers praised
beneath thatched roofs,
whistled in shebeens,
or rippled for lovers on the shore
when wind rushed fear
into the boats of the fish hunter.

I had heard of you
and your difference
that called old men
to your southern place,
where sean-nós moves
strong and natural
as the strange eastern ship
your father built in the haggard.

But only when by accident
I find this room in a city bar
crowded with the listening silence
that your voice evokes,
can I forget your tiny stature,
your loneliness, the arguments
we hated but had, and wonder
instead at the power of you

when you steady yourself
with a chair back,
touch eyelashes
against your cheek bones,
tilt your face high,
and shake rafters
with the loved tradition
of your song.

After, the clap of approval
and gasp of praise.
Maith thú, go h-álainn, ó thuaidh...
and the question always,
Cad as duit?

Where you come from
can only be found
in the secrets of your song
we are lucky to hear.
A rún, a rún,
won't you come back soon,
to the love that is always burning.

Guitar

for Kate Stewart

Music came from behind his fingernails
where the day's dirt was. A hint of face
was visible in his round red beard.
An organ grinder ground to a halt
to listen as the music came
from the tramp's broken silhouette.

And the monkey slowed down to a Viennese waltz.

Soon the street had frozen to a painting:
the baker had stopped baking, the butcher,
bejewelled in a chain of sausages, imagined
the melody drifting delicately down the street
like soap bubbles blown by the old guitar.

Eugene **O'Connell**

Blind Faith

after Guntar Godins

A flute in his hand
He piped an alto march
At the head of the riflemen
Shouting 'long live Stalin'.

Strutting the platform at Riga
After the wind changed and blew
Smoke in the face of the insurgents
He cocked a pistol, closed one eye.

He was farsighted, unlike the apologists
For the Resistance who cited smoke
A chance wind change for their woes
'History is like smoked meat'.

He scoffed, rolling up his sleeves
To rid Latvia of the 'idle influence'
Lugged millstones up hills
Lifted whole orchestras into place.

Unshakable in his faith he'd pounded
At a rock, dust blinded to the grain
Of truth that showed when you peeled
Away the skin of a smiling dictator.

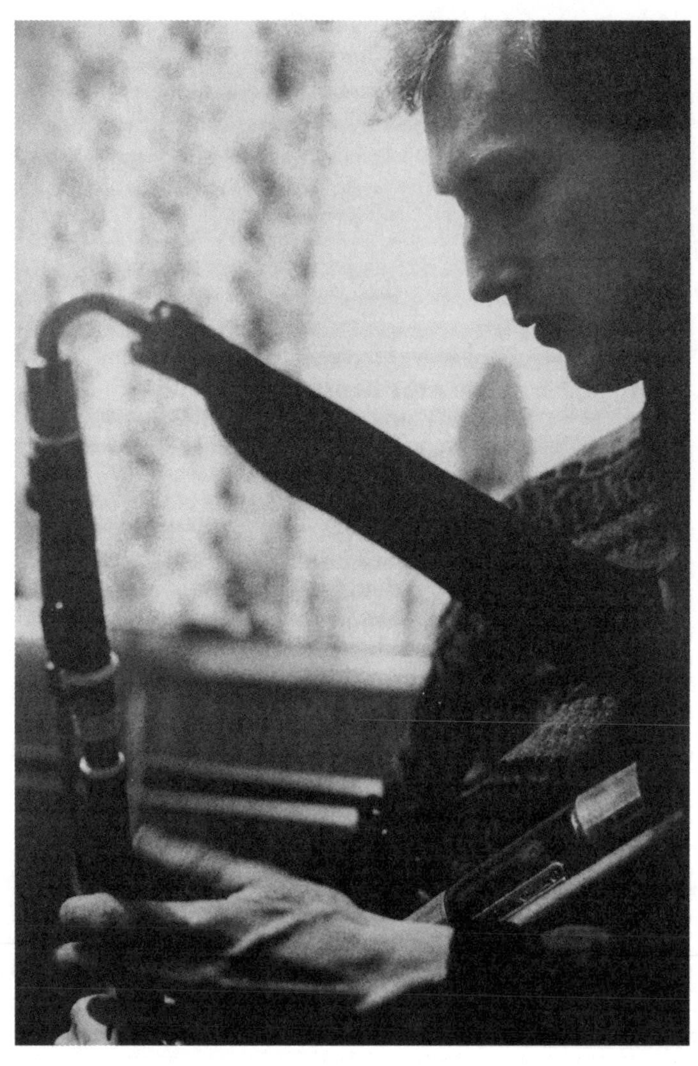

Pete **Mullineaux**

A Piper Prepares

It's almost like shooting up: a captivating ritual –
the belt looped around the forearm; buckle
notched, blowpipe joined to leather bag; a shard
of cloth, folded between elbow and rib for comfort –

trusted talisman, guardian against the unknown
and unnamed – keys, bars with no endings. Drones
are attached like pistol silencers, regulators poised –
and now, the popping strap – the 'piper's apron'

a leather patch, spread across the thigh; you'd think
for protection from the crazed jabs of the chanter,
its manic hypodermic dance. In fact, the placing there
will cause a glottal stop, suspension of sound, a near-

death, allowing trap-door drop, down the pit-shaft
of the octave to low D: belly-forge, base underworld
from where a primal hum vibrates, connects –
fixes on the spinal cord, sends a hit exploding

into the skull's chamber. The head reels, a gasp
for air as the bellows fill and suddenly there's life
in the lungs and wind in the reeds, escape – we're
up and away – tripping over the scales, flying

above the Walls of Limerick, the never ending
Siege of Ennis – hello and goodbye to Rocky Road,
Wheels of the World, Hills and spills of Donegal –
heading towards that high high doh...

A Sad Air's Best for Night

Hofstetter's Serenade

(Máire Ní Chuilleanáin, 1944-1990)

I felt the draught just now as I was keying in the numbers –
the date of her death, going on twenty-five years ago;
it is May but the bright evening is turning colder,
the tight bundle of grief has opened out and spread
wide across these years she knows nothing of, and if I go
in search of her I must unwind and stretch out the thread
she left us, so it twines like a long devious border
turning between the music stands, over and under
the kettledrums and the big bass lying on its side,
but it plunges away leaving the concert-hall behind
and catches her at the start, in the year she was eleven, when
it first rose out of her, the pure line of sound that grows
rising dipping never landing twice on the same spot, then
catching its breath and then flowing along as even
as her own breathing, smooth like a weaver's thread
back and forth tracing. It weaves and it hops again,
the arched finger nails down the note but it overflows.

She was eleven years old. A thousand years before,
she could have been married to an emperor, she was sure
she was able to consent on the spot, as the notes wrapped around her, and
she went on playing as her eyes opened; like words,
like the long serpent that can only swim upstream, like time
the line drew her along, the string and the bow, towards
the moment I saw the breath leaving her body and the silence began.

Chris **Agee**

Nine years

ago
today
your sister
was deathly ill
now
by chance
or happenstance
in St Paul's
under the lantern
and golden gallery
readings and addresses
a string quartet

silence is kept

giving way
or given away
when the cock crows
to the crowds
on this good Friday

'Silence is kept': from the Liturgy
St Paul's Cathedral, London
Good Friday, 2010

Louis de Paor

Rory

Halla na Cathrach, Corcaigh 1976

Milliún míle siar uait
thiar i dtóin an halla,
bhí mo chroí ag bualadh
thiompán mo bhas,
an chruit im chuisle á míniú amach
idir t'ordóg is m'inchinn bhuailte,
gan nóta im cheann
ach an spionnadh a chuiris-se
le sreanganna in achrann.

B'ait liom go raghfá ag tincéireacht
mar sin ar bhuille scoir an tiúin
is tormán ár mbasbhualaidh
ag líonadh fé shála do lámh
a thug snámh smigín dom mhian
ag trácht ar uisce coipthe.

An é nár airís an tuile
ag líonadh ort, rabharta cos
a dhein bord loinge den urlár
i Halla na Cathrach
is ná líonfaidh feasta an poll
a d'fhágais ar ardán id dhiaidh?

An mbraitheann tú anois é,
ár ngile mearluaimneach méar,
is solas na bhflaitheas
ag sluaistiú ciúnais
ar shúile an tslua
atá buailte le stáitse
ag glaoch ar ais ort ón ndoircheacht,
Rory
Rory
Rory

An gcloiseann tú anois ár nguí?

Louis **de Paor**

Rory

Cork City Hall 1976

A million miles away from you
right at the back of the hall
my heart was beating
the drums of my hands;
I hadn't a note in my head
only the grace-notes you picked
from tangled strings
as the knot in my veins
was undone by your brilliant fingers.

I couldn't work out
why you kept tinkering
with the end of the tune
while the roar of our applause
rose up under the heels of your hands
that kept my dreams above water
as you walked the angry sea.

Did you really not hear
the tide flooding in behind you,
the waves of pounding feet
that rocked the floor of the City Hall
until it rolled like the deck of a ship,
that will never fill the emptiness
you left behind you on stage?

Can you feel it now,
our swift-fingered brightness,
as the light of heaven
shovels silence on the eyes
of the crowd as they press against the stage,
calling you back from the dark:
Rory
Rory
Rory...

Now can you hear me?

In Memory: The Miami Showband – Massacred 31 July 1975

Beautiful are the feet of them that preach the gospel of peace,
of them that bring glad tidings of good things

In a public house, darkly lit, a patriotic (sic)
Versifier whines into my face: "You must take one side
Or the other, or you're but a fucking romantic."
His eyes glitter hate and vanity, porter and whiskey,
And I realize that he is blind to the braille connection
Between a music and a music-maker.
"You must take one side or the other
Or you're but a fucking romantic":
The whine is icy
And his eyes hang loose like sheet from poles
On a bare wet hillside in winter
And his mouth gapes like a cave in ice;
It is a whine in the crotch of whose fear
Is fondled a dream gun blood-smeared;
It is in war – not poetry or music –
That men find their niche, their glory hole;
Like most of his fellows
He will abide no contradiction in the mind.
He whines: "If there is birth, there cannot be death"
And – jabbing a hysterical forefinger into my nose and eyes –
"If there is death, there cannot be birth."
Peace to the souls of those who unlike my fellow poet
Were true to their trade
Despite death-dealing blackmail by racists:
You made music, and that was all: You were realists
And beautiful were your feet.

Pearse **Hutchinson**

Ó Riada

Thug tú féin an samhradh leat,
ag dul isteach sa ngeimhreadh dhuit,
ach d'fhágaís féin an samhradh againn
gan fuacht air go deo.

Geimhreadh: cailleadh do cheol féin.
Samhradh do cheoil inár ngleic.

Gréagach i ngéibheann ár ngríosú,
do bhrostaigh, do bhronn meanma;
i bhfuacht na carcrach, blas na gréine;
tú féin i ngéibheann an bháis
(ár gcomharsa béal-dorais)
ag seinm samhraidh. Ár múscailt.

Ó Riada

You took the summer with you,
as you went into the winter,
but you left the summer with us,
banishing the cold.

Winter: your own music lost.
But the summer of your music is ours.

A Greek in prison kept our hearts up,
he quickened us, lent hope;
in prison-cold, a taste of sun;
you now in the prison of death
(our next-door neighbour)
performing summer. Waking us up.

Leland **Bardwell**

Outside the Odeon, Camden Town

The snow on the street like stewed apple
the buses slopslopping past
with carton-loads of Paddies.
In the illuminated cheek-bones
of the Odeon cinema
on my twenty-ninth birthday I waited.

An aeroplane took off in Arizona
and Buddy Holly died.

Last week Elvis Presley
felt his chest grip the skin – felt
his shrivelled parts like an empty money belt
quiver for the last time.

I am not weeping for an old star's death
or a man stumbling in secrecy
to an appointment with a mediocre end
but myself gone forty-nine with memories
of my first record player and a bunch
of 45s and a Greek boy separating air from vowels:

'Will you come…ba-by…will you come?'

Leland **Bardwell**

Insomnia

With me in my truckle bed
There is a hound
A hound in my head
There is no gainsaying it
It howls

It is the lesson of darkness

Oh Couperin
Couperin le Grand

Michael **Longley**

Words for Jazz Perhaps

for Solly Lipsitz

Elegy for Fats Waller

Lighting up, lest our hearts should break,
His fiftieth cigarette of the day,
Happy with so many notes at his beck
And call, he sits there taking it away,
The maker of immaculate slapstick.

With music and with such precise rampage
Across the deserts of the blues a trail
He blazes, towards the one true mirage,
Enormous on a nimble-footed camel
And almost refusing to be his age.

He plays for hours on end and though there be
Oases one part water, two parts gin,
He tumbles past to reign, wise and thirsty,
At the still centre of his loud dominion –
THE SHOOK THE SHAKE THE SHEIK OF ARABY:

Bud Freeman in Belfast

Foghorn and factory siren intercept
Each fragile hoarded-up refrain. What else
Is there to do but let those notes erupt

Until your fading last glissando settles
Among all other sounds – carefully wrapped
In the cotton wool from aspirin bottles?

To Bessie Smith

You bring from Chattanooga Tennessee
Your huge voice to the back of my mind
Where, like sea shells salvaged from the sea
As bright reminders of a few weeks' stay,
Some random notes are all I ever find.
I couldn't play your records every day.

I think of Tra-na-rossan, Inisheer,
Of Harris drenched by horizontal rain –
Those landscapes I must visit year by year.
I do not live with sounds so seasonal
Nor set up house for good. Your blues contain
Each longed-for holiday, each terminal.

To Bix Beiderbecke

In hotel rooms, in digs you went to school.
These dead were voices from the floor below
Who filled like an empty room your skull,

Who shared your perpetual one-night stand
– The havoc there, and the manoeuvrings! –
Each coloured hero with his instrument.

You were bound with one original theme
To compose in your head your terminus,
Or to improvise with the best of them

That parabola from blues to barrelhouse.

Salt Fields

Air: St James Infirmary

Well if you call and still can't hear me
Don't put the blame on me
Here where I always have been
In the salt fields of the sea

Well we got here way too early
An hour before dawn or so
The market houses still not open
Nowhere else to go

We believe we're somehow stronger
And wiser than before
But I know it's all delusion
And whatever else we were

If you lose her you'll never find her
Nothing but desire
That chains you to the madman
And the ash of last night's fire

Again I hear the loud dawn chorus
Another night has gone
Melted in the blue of the morning
And the great wide world spins on

Well if you call and still can't hear me
Don't put the blame on me
Here where I always have been
In the salt fields of the sea

Hugh **Maxton**

War and Music

for the late Geoffrey King

The drum rolls through history,
Tattoos and sundry punctures,
Bugle calls, beats, raps and bars,
Death rattles *da capo*.

To care-free beholders,
The viola-cellist leans
Like an exhausted soldier.
'Listen (you said) without hearing.'

Sensualdo, the lutenist,
Murdered his wife and her lover;
Exposed their naked bodies
On the ringing steps.

McCormack, it is hinted,
In youth had a rival snuffed out
The better to better
His unrivalled *bel canto*.

The Terezin chamber trio
Played to packed houses.
Its entrepreneur ordered
Escape from the Seraglio.

When the emperor died
Young Ludwig wrote a
Cantata buried
For technical difficulty.

It is possible to believe
Music
Unaccompanied by word,
Voice, photograph or god.

Tolstoy wept at a string quartet
(2nd movement
Andante cantabile),
Then ordered his peasants

To replace all the snow
Dug from an endless avenue
Through *Woods of the Old Order*
For their master's greater ease.

Paula **Meehan**

Home

I am the blind woman finding her way home by a map of tune.
When the song that is in me is the song I hear from the world
I'll be home. It's not written down and I don't remember the words.
I'll know when I hear it I'll have made it myself. I'll be home.

A version I heard once in Leitrim was close, a wet Tuesday night
in the Sean Relig bar. I had come for the session, I stayed
for the vision and lore. The landlord called time,
the music dried up, the grace notes were pitched to the dark.
When the jukebox blared out *I'd only four senses and he left me senseless*,
I'd no choice but to take to the road. On Grafton Street in November
I heard a mighty sound: a travelling man with a didgeridoo
blew me clear to Botany Bay. The tune too far back to live in
but scribed on my bones. In a past life I may have been Kangaroo
rocked in my dreamtime, convict ships coming o'er the foam.

In the Puzzle Factory one winter I was sure I was home.
The talking in tongues, the riddles, the rhymes, struck a chord
that cut through the pharmaceutical haze. My rhythm catatonic,
I lulled myself back to the womb, my mother's heart
beating the drum of herself and her world. I was tricked
by her undersong, just close enough to my own. I took then
to dancing; I spun like a Dervish. I swear I heard the subtle
music of the spheres. It's no place to live, but –
out there in space, on your own, hung aloft the night.
The tune was in truth a mechanical drone;
I was a pitiful monkey jigging on cue. I came back to earth
with a land, to rain on my face, to sun in my hair. And grateful, too.

The wisewomen say you must live in your skin, call *it* home,
no matter how battered and broken, misused by the world, you
can heal.
This morning a letter arrived on the nine o'clock post.
The Department of Historical Reparation, and who did I blame?
The Nuns? Your Mother? The State? *Tick box provided,*
we'll consider your case. I'm burning my soapbox, I'm taking
the very next train. A citizen of nowhere, nothing to my name.

I'm on my last journey. Though my lines are all wonky
they spell me a map that makes sense. Where the song that is in me
is the song I hear from the world, I'll set down my burdens
and sleep. The spot that I lie on at last the place I'll call home.

Grief

stumbles
in black gloves
down unlit cul-de-sacs
where words silt up in drifts –
spilt tesserae,
redundant letters
that can no longer find their way
or seek each other out to spell
how did it come to this?

Grief wavers
on the indrawn breath
of a day not yet begun,
in a shroud of mist unsettled
by the rummage of birds;

breaks
on the grace note
of a wren.

John **Montague**

Lullaby

from *Flower, Stone, Sea*

3 September 1963

great sea-mother, your voice
is monotonous! I sat beside
you for a whole day, trying
to speak of a friend's death,
but all that you answered
was one single word,
with its many variations...S-h-u-s-h.

In your Sleep

after *The Lark Ascending* by Vaughan Williams

The moment the lark finally vanishes
into the spread green sky of the forest
is the moment you suddenly lift

your bruised arm up, over your body,
as though to show me the wing's eclipse,
or the wing, or the season of your dream.

And even as your hand lapses silent
onto your chest, and your breath goes
sluggish, I am already watching your feet

prepare their slow first step under the sheet
as the last notes of sunlight fall quiet,
and you do not move again. Oh my dreamer,

are you a bird reviving in a summer field?
Was it the lark ascending that you heard,
a ghost among its shy-hearted tunes?

Yes. I heard the lark escaping, too.

Dennis **O'Driscoll**

Nocturne, Op. 2

A sad air's best for night as you mope about
the house, closing windows, checking doors.
Slow, cumulative strokes of the violin bow,
the most ruminative notes that can be coaxed
from the cello, nocturnes unlocked by black piano keys.

Strains that are trained directly on the heart
when its resistance sinks, like temperatures,
to a day's-end low: music that tells of how
things stand in the troubled world you now have
in your hands to potter about in on your own.

Music of the kind whose fearful darkness would
unnerve you as a child, but whose darkness
seems the very point, this late night here, a slow
movement's stark conclusion ringing sadly true.

Moya **Cannon**

Lament

Let me learn from the Brent geese
their grey grammar of grief
as they wheel in a bow-backed flock
onto a February tide.

Let me learn from these strong geese
to map my losses with a cry,
learn from those who are always losing
a chick, a lover or a brother,
losing one cold country or another.

Let me learn from the black-necked geese
how to bend my shoulders low
over a wrack-draped shore,
let me learn from the curlew's long weep,
Oh, oh, oh, oh, oh.

Colm **Tóibín**

excerpt from ***Everything is Susceptible***

There were a few moments in the stately slow movement of the Bach Violin Concerto playing on the stereo that made her stop what she was doing at the computer and move across the room and stand at the window. Maybe there would come a time in the future, she thought, a time after birdsong, a time when thunder and the sound of rain were faint memories, when music too would be obsolete, when the word 'music' would be a dead word, or a metaphor for something, and no one would know how to conjure up this sound that came from the two speakers planted on either side of the long shelf. It would be a time when most violins themselves had been chopped up for firewood and burned, or been left to rot, and the surviving ones put on show in museums, admired eventually for their strangeness, with notices beside them explaining that once, it was presumed, they may have contained relics of the saints or the Hollywood stars.

All that would remain of this music, then, she imagined, would be a photo someone had taken once of a CD itself, the lovely smooth silver side reflecting the light, but the photo would be of just a small area of it, the part where fragments of the chords that had caught her attention were buried deep, or were, for all she knew, actually contained in the silver. Maybe they had once been part of a single sound, the stable sound of the world itself, and had been scattered into melody by the composer. In the future, it struck her, the composing of the music might be seen as part of a neurosis that had now been cured, or might be viewed as something unlucky, something which had merely caused harm.
(...)
Three years before she died, Elisabeth Bishop published her last book which contained just nine poems. Her previous book of new poems had been published eleven years earlier. While she left many poems unpublished or incomplete, she wrote only nine poems which fully satisfied her in those eleven years between 1965 and 1976.

As our artist looks through the CDs, she thinks about this, the space between Bishop's poems, days of silence, revision, days when nothing much was done. She almost chooses a CD of piano music by Debussy, but thinks better of it. She remembers that Elisabeth Bishop listened with fascination to music by Anton Webern, music which sounds like something distilled, like whispers, with traces of melody. She finds a CD of his chamber music and puts it on and then takes down a book of Bishop's poems so she can look at what Bishop did in those last nine poems.

Bishop, it seems to her as she reads, was interested in the relationship between something, a thing made, or an identity, and the nothing much that lay behind it, or the little that would be its fate. In the first poem in that last book, the poet, a young girl aged almost seven, realised that she actually existed, that she was a person apart from others, and that she always would be. The poet could not find a word for this realisation, and then the word came, the word was 'unlikely', how 'unlikely' it was.

And then the matter of size. How big we are in relation to some things, and how small when compared to others. As the music played, our artist put the book of poems aside for a moment and took down some of the souvenirs she had gathered of towers and monuments and held them in her hands as though she were a giant and could decide their fate. Elisabeth Bishop, too, contemplated the world as too small or too large, the world, for example, as viewed by Robinson Crusoe in Bishop's poem 'Crusoe in England'. On the island there were volcanoes:

> I'd think that if they were the size
> I thought volcanoes should be, then I had
> become a giant

In 'Night City', Bishop watched the minuscule world from a plane. And in '12 O'Clock News' she viewed her desk as a war zone. Her lamp was the moon, her typewriter an escarpment, her typed sheet either an airstrip or a cemetery, her ashtray a nest of soldiers.

And then at the beginning of the poem 'The End of March', on a beach, there were dog-prints so big that they could have been lion-prints, and then 'lengths and lengths, endless, of wet white string'. The poet did not know what it was. 'A kite string? – But no kite.'

*

The music from the speakers moves into silence now, exudes a feeling that there must have been more music at one time, but it was cut away, scattered. Maybe it will be found orbiting the earth, maybe the notes that Webern discarded did not go to waste. No one is listening to them, and that may be what they were for. In the meantime, by the end of her poem, Elizabeth Bishop has found nothing new but she has dreamed a bit and then turned and retraced her steps on the beach. Retracing her own steps – the other way around of course – she imagines the 'lion sun':

> – a sun who'd walked the beach the last low tide,
> making those big majestic paw-prints,
> who perhaps had batted a kite out of the sky to play with.

It occurs to our artist now this morning in her living room with the computer still open in front of her, as the piano plays some notes and then seems to think better of it, that the world she had created, the one she has been playing with for years – half-drowning tiny versions of monuments in bathwater, for example, or sending meteorites back into the sky as fireworks, or conjuring up new ways to unsee the world, unravel its past, unrepresent its contours, unmake objects – has been closer to the dark truth lurking at the edge of things, closer to history and knowledge and the great silence to come than even she, when she was visited by this visions, had ever imagined.

Michael **Longley**

Madame Butterfly

Through atmospherics I hear you die again.
Death is white as your lover's uniform, as snow
When it covers the whiteness of almond petals.
Worse weather blows your papery house away.
Now listen for the snow bunting's arrival,
A flute-note from crevices and rocky scree.

Thomas McCarthy

Scriabin's Piano Sonata No. 2 in G sharp minor, Op. 19

Russia that has suddenly become famous all over again;
Famous, that is, for famously not giving a damn,
Has given me this exquisite Welte-Mignon piano-roll
Of Alexander Scriabin going up in arpeggios of flames
As if the ivories of his Moscow piano pierced the soul
Of something God-like in a cold studio. It always begins
With a dark art of something unexpected and bass,
Reversing over time into the sweetest Andante, as if
Just to talk to a bear would give the composer peace;
The composer in this case being an excited pianist,
Listening to no one, letting the melodies run adrift
To settle like a heavy tank in a distant wheat-field. My heart
Is in my mouth, yet again. This room is covered in a mist
Of war. Don't die young, I say. Oh, pianist, don't start.

Eva **Bourke**

The Irish tenor Michael Kelly recalls Mozart in Paris

How could I forget him – wrapped in his greatcoat
against the icy blasts as he strode past the liveried
hauteur of tall gates, first citizen of the republic
of music, a small figure, nondescript,
with bulging eyes, as the poet Tieck depicted
him, or picking his way through stench and dirt
of Paris streets, an immigré rehearsing the words
for coldness of heart in the local argot.

They kept him waiting for hours
in freezing ante-rooms, in arctic salons
while his fingers turned numb, gave him out of tune
clavichords, the lords and ladies turning deaf ears;
when he played only the armchairs
and walls listened. Years before Paris had begun with
so much promise. Fingers on the keyboard, his,
his sister's, Piano Sonata for four hands. *Divine*,

they gushed, *a mere child*, C-Major, the key
of light. To this day I see him hurry
through the dark winter streets, snow
powdering his wig, shoulders, through muddy lanes,
past candelabra aflicker in tall windows,
his mother dying in the hotel. *Prego,*
di pardonarmi, carissima, he wrote. (The irony
of today's plaque: *Mozart et sa mère séjournèrent ici.*)

He did all he could but *failed to please.*
No, he was not a great success,
the Parisian Symphony, fireworks and fanfares
for Legros and stupid donkeys that lacked ears.
Dear father, I could do nothing in this place
of coldness, her wrote to Leopold. Always he fell
short, always he apologized. Paris
was a flop, his name at the end of a long playbill.

But whenever I sang Tamino's aria '*Dies Bildnis*
ist bezaubernd schön...' it was inexplicable,
and – forgive the cliché – unearthly, a work of genius.
What its mystery is? Who can tell?
Perhaps the melody's naked appeal
to the heart. Yes, he talked of an emptiness that pains.
Destitute, he was still able to be pleased
that his dear 'Papa Haydn' was féted in England.

And in the end? he was drained,
sick of playing the clown –
his canto *funèbre*? he had to leave it undone.

Ted **Deppe**

The Funeral March of Adolf Wölfli

from the oral history of Lisa Becker taken in Berne, Switzerland, 1970.

I found that art would keep him quiet. After breaking
a fellow patient's wrist, he was isolated for years

– I brought him coloured pencils and newsprint
and he drew all day, or composed music in a system

God revealed to him. For a time he thought he loved me.
For a time my face appeared in every drawing he made.

He wrote the 'Santa Lisa Polka' for me, hardly danceable, but –
despite the homemade paper trumpet he hummed on –

haunting, and mine. He said, once, if I married him,
he'd abdicate his kingdom, write a waltz for me each day.

Strange, then, after he died, to search in vain
through his eight-thousand-page *Funeral March*, looking

for something – anything – I could play before we buried him.
His masterpiece reached to the ceiling of his cell,

hand-sewn scores in which the music constantly gave way
to drawings or ads from magazines. What might have been

eighth notes floated above maps or rambling prayers,
and then staves appeared with no notes at all –

this was the work he'd curse me for disturbing!
The night before his funeral, I sorted through

those composition books and found no sustained melody –
but what did I expect? When he worked, he had a ritual

of rolling up his shirtsleeves and trousers
that took hours, interrupted by his voices. He'd start

drawing in the margins and press inward, filling each space,
singing to himself like a boy. Oh, he was more selfish

than a child, incapable of loving anyone. I never told him
I wasn't married. I took care of him thirty years, longer

than most marriages last! Such a strange, ugly fellow –
our yellow-fingered, warp-nailed, one-man Renaissance.

He'd consume his week's supply of pencils in three days,
then beg for more – against the doctor's orders I gave them.

His *March* was signed, 'St. Adolf, Chief Music Director,
Painter, Writer, Inventor of 160 Highly Valuable Inventions,

Victor of Mammoth Battles, Alright!! Giant-Theatre-Director,
Great God, Mental Patient, Casualty'.

In some ways I was relieved when he died, as if a blizzard
finally howled away and I could start to shovel out.

He didn't want to leave a few perfect works behind.
He wanted to lift up everything, wanted to give

the whole dying world lasting form.
There were lucid moments when he knew he was mad –

he could almost imagine what a normal life might be.
I'd go home and practise piano every night.

I'd play Beethoven, feel the moments things caught fire,
but couldn't myself become flame.

Page upon page of his *March*, containing, he said, everything
and everyone he'd ever loved, and not a single tune

I could play for his funeral. Not even the 'Santa Lisa Polka'.
We buried him without music. There is nothing

I blame myself for more. We buried him without music
and for two weeks I took to bed. Then one night –

it was snowing – I rolled up the sleeves of my nightdress.
I pinned up the hem, then puzzled over a line of music

that vanished in a field of painted irises, purple flags
instead of notes waving under a sky of sharps and flats.

I closed my eyes and began to play. I didn't know
what my hands were doing. Snow kept falling,

silences tumbled forward, winged notes soared
above chipped ivory keys. I played what I could

of his *Funeral March* – imperfectly, of course,
only in fragments – I played the *Funeral March*

of Adolf Wölfli, everything dark, falling, silver.

Eugene **O'Connell**

Letters from Africa

I had to stack the letters
Against a briar, like the folds
Of a melodeon, that I pulled
Towards me to make a draught,
To redden the envelopes that
Were so fine when you posted them
I had to cut them with a blade,
In case I'd have to stitch any word
That I had missed with Sellotape.
Now the red white and blue edges
Of your letters from Africa are burning
In my backyard, and no matter
How much I prime the bellows
Of my makeshift melodeon
I can't knock a tune out of it.

On the Pier

The yellow of a lake in Autumn
Washes my eyes, clarifies.
A breeze blows open the pages
Of the album you gave me.
Time passes, so I'm not sure
If it was your eyes, hair or mouth
That had the peculiar colour of smoke.
Sorrow is a mood: the lake lifts,
The geese with undercarriage down
Coming in to land, the sound
Of a flute carrying over the water.

Julie **O'Callaghan**

Saturday Afternoon in Dublin

Dietrich Fischer-Dieskau is in the process
of depressing me singing
the 'Der Einsame im Herbst' section
of *Das Lied von der Erde*.
A flute is playing as I look
at my sisters photographed in New York
in a crowd of twenty-five thousand people
getting ready for a bicycle tour.
I meet them for a few days
every two years or so
but I don't know them anymore;
only how they used to be
before I went away.
Are you crying yet?
Sometimes you get to know your relatives
better when they're pinned down
like butterfly specimens
wearing baseball cap and crash helmet respectively.
Kate, I see, has a blue-faced watch
with snappy red band.
Ellen has let her hair grow.
They both smile nervously
because my father is taking the picture
in the middle of the throng.
Dietrich, meanwhile, has moved on to a beautiful, sad,
song with harps – I'm glad I don't know any German –
it's even sadder hearing words sung
that make no sense.
He says, 'Ja, ja' better than anyone.
It isn't music for New York, really.
A Hopper etching: 'Night Shadows',
an afternoon in Dublin looking
out the arid window for inspiration,
wanting so many things to happen –
that's when it gets to you.
Are you crying yet?

John McAuliffe

At a Concert

'Throughout the ravishing sestet he composed poems.' – Richard Outram

He reaches for a scrap of paper as the crowd files in,
fumbling it out of an overcoat beneath the flip-up seat.
The quartet, in their appointed places, tune up: he keeps
to himself the feeling this might be the part

he will enjoy the most. Tall, rumpled, all in black,
the composer is the image of a curate who kept him behind,
in the sacristy, one morning to count collection money.
The arresting opening bar strikes home and he feels

not at all bad, singled out even, though he worries
as the counterpoint continues, if that pain
coming into focus in his right eye is a scratch, he hopes not,
or a sty, which would be painful – he turns off his phone –

given the week he has ahead, the flights, there and back,
seeing his family, long journeys he'd like to read through.
But the half-stripped hallway and dented car, he arches his neck,
are on his mind and he wishes this passage would end

as he notices the light seeming to shift behind the cellist
gathered around her instrument like a slept-in coat,
and a familiar colour shines in the half-lit front row
which he forgets, responding to the cellist's

sudden frenzied relieving response to the violins' permutations.
In Niagara once, by himself, he photographed the spray
and a boat that circled and almost tipped over, knowing
behind him stood gewgaw stalls from which he'd take something away,

thinking of this, as the applause starts, unprepared, eyes abrim,
someone had said, yes, there would be no interval,
so this was it, over before he was ready, and around him,
in the rustling coats, the shifting sounds of conversation.

David **Wheatley**

from ***Sonnets to Robert Fergusson (1750–1774)***

Ane place ye'll hear a lassie's voice is sangschaws *one* *song-shows/concerts*
doon The Blue Lamp: 'There lived twa sisters
in ane bower...'. Songs whaur hairt-wae festers *heartbreak*
wi' unfinished business, sair and anxious. *sore*
And someone's for the chop: 'He's coorted the eldest
wi' his penknife...' But then she kills the younger
quine for spite, wha'd ne'er done ocht to wrong her.
Songs that chowk the dulie lungs like coal-dust. *sad*
You'd a braw voice for your 'Lassie My Dearie', *fine*
but a maiden in song is soon unmade:
the hairt's mair slauchterhoose than nunnery. *heart*
Strike up while you can wi' 'Lassie Lie Near Me',
but ballads want blood: 'There's either a maid
or a milk-white swan drooned in the dams of Minorie.'

Burnfort, Las Vegas

We move the Sacred Heart lamp
closer to Elvis's face now in the
month of June. I think that those
billboards of Vegas
could be the Major cigarette sign
or the Double Diamond Works Wonders
in the lounge window round '75
or the BP pump shining in
the blue Burnfort evening,
the wood pigeons cooing
as the men come down from
the mountain and fill their vans
with petrol – a violet cloud with
a tantalizing smell and someone
says Burnfort is like New York
to those mountainy men the way
it is all built up with a school
and a church and a post office and us
city slickers running the pub,
shop and petrol pumps
and I believe it is true,
that we are like that to them –
there were stranger things then
to believe in only now I think
it was more like Vegas, all those
signs, the games of forty five
and my Elvis tape playing.
A few months ago,
the novelty mug frightened us all
by spontaneously bursting
into Viva Las Vegas and I took that
as a sign, did what any
Catholic would do – put up a shrine.

Martina **Evans**

Elvis is Dying

Well you may run on for a long time
Run on for a long time,
Run on for a long time
Let me tell you God Almighty's gonna cut you down

This Dalston winter morning, I can stop time
put down the biography
look out at the back garden where
the frost powders the vine twigs
it's 35 degrees in Memphis, he hasn't gone
to the bathroom yet. I take a look out
the front through frost-blackened
fuchsia – Balls Pond Road,
the woman in full adidas, the man in the truck tapping
the steering wheel, the seagull as big as a cat?
When I pick up the book again
he's walking into the big red bathroom,
with the black toilet, the chair in the shower. Ginger
sleeps through the Memphis heat, she will put on her make-up
before she checks on him, to the outrage of the eternal millions
crowding round the windows of Graceland
searching YouTube for his dappled shadow
flitting through that antebellum mansion. Behind
my grille of black twigs, I turn the page,
he's down in his face in his own vomit
and I remember his namesake
that tinker from Cork, Elvis O'Donnell –
strange to think, he died in a ditch in the very same way.

Ken **Bruen**

To Have To Hold

"I should have married Johnny Cash."
The cop was taken aback. Of all the things he expected her to say, this was never on the table.
He looked at her, the dishwater blond hair, the hard mouth, the slight, jagged scar along her cheek and the air of exhaustion she exuded. The coffee he'd sent out for was before her and she moved her manacled hands to take a sip, the Styrofoam cup tilted back, and he glimpsed very white teeth. He had her statement before him and if he could just get her to sign the goddamn thing, he might beat the gridlock, get home to supper before eight. His partner had gone for a leak and the tape recorder had been shut off.
She raised her hands, asked, "Y'all could maybe take these off for a time?" He could see where the metal had cut into her wrists and angry welts ran along the bone. He said, "Now, Charlene, you know I gotta keep you cuffed 'til booking is done."
She sighed, then asked,
"Got a smoke?"
He had a pack of Kools in his suit pocket, for his wife, shook his head, said,
"No smoking in a Federal building, you know that."
She gave him a smile and it lit up her whole face, took twenty years right off her. She said,
"I won't tell if you don't."
And what the hell, he took out the pack and a battered Zippo. It had the logo, "First Airborne." He slid them across the table and she grabbed them, got one in her mouth, cranked the lighter, the smell of gasoline emanating like scarce comfort. She peered at the pack, Menthol, asked, "What's with that, you're not a pillow-biter are you? Not that I have anything against Gays but I can read folk. I'd have you down for a ladies man."
He nearly smiled, thinking,
"Yeah, right."
In his crumpled suit, gray skin, sagging belly, he was a Don Juan. What was it his daughter would answer … Not.
She wasn't expecting an answer, said,
"Years back, I was working one of those fancy hotels, still living high on the hog, and I ran the bar.

Guess who walked in, with his band?"
Her eyes shining at the memory, she continued,
"The Man in Black, he'd done a concert and they dropped in for a few quiet brews and some chicken wings."
Foley was impressed. He liked Cash, except for that prison crap he did, and in spite of himself, asked,
"No shit, the Man himself?"
She was nodding, the smoke like a halo around her head, said,
"I couldn't believe it, I never seen anyone famous, not, like, in real life. I gave 'em my best service, and in those days, I was hot, had some moves."
Foley nearly said, "You still do."
But bit down and wondered where the hell his partner had got to. Probably gone for a bourbon, Shiner back. He'd return, smelling of mints, like that was a disguise. He asked,
"You talk to him, to Mr. Cash?"
"Not at first. I was getting them vittles, drinks, making sure they were comfortable and after, I dunno, an hour, Johnny said, 'Take a pew little lady, get a load off.'"
She rubbed here eyes, then.
"He had these amazing boots, all scuffed but, like, real expensive, snakeskin or something, and he used his boot to hook a chair, pull it up beside him."
She touched her face, self-conscious, said,
"I didn't have the scar then, still had some dreams. Jesus."
Foley was a cop for fifteen years, eight with Homicide and he was, in his own cliché, hard-bitten. There wasn't a story, a scam, an excuse, a smoke screen he hadn't heard and his view of human nature veered from cynical to incredulity. But something about this broad … a sense of, what…? He didn't want to concede it, but was it … dignity? A few months later, a Saturday night, his wedding anniversary, he'd taken his Lottie for clams and that white wine she loved. Had a few too many glasses himself – that shit crept up on you – and told Lottie about the feeling and Lottie had gotten that ice look. He wouldn't be having any lovemaking that night; she hissed,
"You had a shine for that…that trailer trash?"
His night had gone south.
And c'mon, he hadn't got a thing for Charlene, but something, her face now, in the middle of the Cash story, it got to him, she was saying,
"I sat down and Mr. Cash, he asked me my name, I done told him and he repeated it but with an S … like … Shur… leen.

He had that voice, the gravel. Luckies and corn whiskey melt, give a girl the shivers, and then he said, 'That's a real purty name … how he said pretty.'"
She massaged her right wrist, the welt coming in red and inflamed. She said, "I had me a leather thong on my wrist. My Mamma done give it to me, real fancy, little symbols of El Paso interwoven on there, and I dunno, I saw him look at it and maybe it was the heat, it was way up in them there 90s, even that time of the evening, and I took it off, said, 'Can I give you this?'
His boys went quiet for a moment, the longnecks left untouched and them fellers could drink. He took it, tied it on his wrist, gave me that smile, sent goose bumps all down my spine, said, 'Muchas gracias, senorita.'
Then I noticed one of the guys give a start and I turned and June Carter came in, that bitch, full of wrath. Dame had a hard on so I got my ass in gear, got back behind the bar. They didn't stay long after, and Johnny never came to say goodbye, that cow had him bundled out of there like real urgent business. The manager, he come over to the bar, paid the tab and gave me one hundred dollars for my own self. What do you think of that, one hundred bucks, for like, real little service?"
Foley knew hookers. For fifteen minutes, they'd be lucky to get thirty and change. Charlene's face got ugly, a coldness from her eyes, mixed with … grief? She said,
"I was on a high, floating, my face burning, like I was some goddamn teenager, and not even that Carter cunt …".
The word was so unexpected and especially from a woman, that Foley physically moved back, re-considered the handcuffs. Charlene finished with,
"I was cleaning the table, them good ol' boys sure done a mess of wings and longnecks and there … in the middle of the table, sliced neatly in half, was my Mama's wrist band."
A silence took over the room, she fired up another Kool, taking long inhales like she was stabbing her body, her eyes but slits in her face and she said,
"When I'd be clearing up, I'd been humming, I Walk the Line."
Years after, Johnny came on the juke, the radio, that tune, Foley would have to turn it off.
Go figure.

***

When Foley's partner got back, minted almighty, his face with that bourbon glow, he brought some sodas and if he noticed the cuffs were off, he let it slide, turned on the tape recorder, asked,

"You grew up in El Paso, am I right?"

Charlene gave him a look, a blend of amusement and malice, said,

"Cinco de Mayo."

He looked at Foley, shrugged, and Charlene took a slug of the soda, grimaced, asked,

"No Dr. Pepper?"

Then,

"Damn straight, between Stanton and Kansas, you get to the bus station? ... Turn right on Franklin, walk, like maybe a block-and-a-half? ... Little side street there, we had us our place, me and my Mom, near the Gardner Hotel. That building is, like, eighty years old?"

Foley's partner gave a whistle, said,

"No shit?"

Like he could give a fuck.

Foley was pissed at him, felt the interview had gone downhill since he had joined them. Something like intimacy had been soiled, and he had to shake himself, get rid of those damn foolish notions. Charlene stared at him, asked,

"I know he's Foley. Who are you?"

"Darlin', I'm either your worst nightmare or your only hope, comprende Chiquita?"

She tasted the insult, the loaded use of the Spanish, then said,

"No me besas mas, por favor!"

He didn't get it, said,

"I don't get it."

She laughed, said,

"The next whore sits on your face, ask her."

He leant fast across the table, slapped her mouth, hard, and Foley, went,

"Jesus, Al."

His fingers left an outline on her cheek and she smiled.

The week after, when Al asked his regular hooker for a translation, she told him, "Please don't kiss me."

Foley wound back the tape, couldn't have the slap on there, then asked, "So what brought you back to Houston?"
She shrugged, said,
"A guy, what else."
Foley looked at his notes, double-checked, then,
"That'd be the deceased, one Charles Newton?"
She lit up the cigarette she'd been toying with, blew a cloud of smoke at Al, said,
"Charlie, yeah, he promised me he'd marry me, and he was into me for Five Gs."
Al gave a nasty chuckle, more a cackle, asked,
"The matter with you broads, you give your dollars to any lowlife that says he'll marry you?"
She looked away, near whispered,
"He had a voice like Johnny Cash."
Al spread his hands in the universal gesture of the fuck does that mean? Charlene was thinking of her third day in Houston: one of those sudden rainstorms hit and she ducked into a building. Turned out it was a library and she looked to see if maybe they had a book on Johnny. Passing a Literature section, she saw a title ... To Have and Have Not.
For some reason, she read it as To Have and To Hold and was about to open it when the librarian approached, a spinster in her severe fifties, demanded,
"Are you a member, Miss?"
A hiss riding point on the Miss. Charlene knew the type – the dried up bitter fruit of T.V. dinners and vicious cats.
Charlene dropped the book, said,
"If you have anything to do with it, I'm so fucking out of here."
And was gone.
She'd have asked Foley about the book if Al wasn't there, but she shut it down. Charlie was the usual loser she'd always attracted, but he had an apartment near Rice University and she was running out of time, looks and patience. When she caught him going through her purse, she'd finally figured, "What the hell?"
And knifed the bastard, in the neck. Then it felt so good, she stuck him a few more times ... twenty five in all, or so they said. What, they counted? She was still holding the blade when the cops showed up and it was, as they say, a slam-dunk.

Foley said,
"You turned down the offer to have an attorney present."
She gave him what amounted to a tender smile, said,
"They'd assign some guy, and you know what? I'm sick to my gut of men."
Al was unrolling a stick of Juicy Fruit, popped it in his mouth, made some loud sucking noises, said,
"You're a lesbian, that it? Hate all men?"
She let out a breath, said,
"If I sign this, can I get some sleep, some chow?"
Foley passed over a pen, said,
"Have you some ribs, right away."
She signed and Al said,
"Now the bad news darlin'. Ol' Charles, he was the son of a real prominent shaker right here in Houston. Bet he didn't tell you that. You're going away for a long time."
She stretched, asked,
"And what makes you think I give a fuck?"

***

She got fifteen years. As she was being led down, Al leaned over, said,
"Come sundown, a bull dyke's gonna make you think of Johnny Cash in a whole new light."
She spat in his face.
Six months later, Foley went to see her. He didn't tell Al. When they brought her into the interview room, he was shocked by her appearance. Her frame had shrunk int itself and her eyes were hollow, but she managed a weak smile, said,
"Detective, what brings you out to see the gals?"
He was nervous, his hands awash with sweat, and he blamed the humidity, asked,
"They treating you okay?"
She laughed, said,
"Like one of their own."
He produced a pack of Kools and a book of matches.
She looked at him, said,
"I quit."
He felt foolish, tried,
"You can use them for barter, maybe?"
She had a faraway expression in her eyes, near whispered,

"They got nothing I want."
He had a hundred questions he wanted to ask, but couldn't think how to frame them and stared at the table. She reached over, touched his hand, said,
"Johnny was on T.V. last week, did a song called Hurt, he sang that for me."
Then she changed tack, said,
"You ever get to El Paso and want to cross the border, take the number 10 green trolley to The Santa Fe Bridge. Don't take The Border Jumper Trolley – it's, like, real expensive. Walk to the right side of The Stanton Bridge and it's twenty-five cents to cross and in El Paso, you want some action, go to The Far West Rodeo, on Airways Boulevard. They sometimes got live rodeo, and hey, get a few brews in, you might even try the mechanical bull, that's a riot."
Relieved to have something to talk about, he asked,
"You went there a lot?"
"Never, not one time. But I heard, you know?"
He looked at his watch and she said,
"Y'all better be getting on, I got to write me a letter to Johnny, let him know where I'm at."
Foley was standing and said,
"Charlene, he's dead. He died last week."
For a moment, she was stock still, then she emitted a howl of anguish that brought the guards running. She wailed,
"You fucking liar – he's not dead. He'll never be dead to me – how do you think I get through this hell?"
As he hurried down the cellblock, he could still hear her screams, his sweat rolling in rivulets, creasing his cheap suit even further.
As he got his car in "drive," he reached in his jacket, took out the packaged C.D. of Johnny's Greatest Hits … slung it out the window, the disc rolling along the desert for a brief second, then coming to a stop near some sagebrush.
A rodent tearing at the paper exposed Cash's craggy face, and, viewed in a certain light, you'd think he was looking towards the prison.
Impossible to read his expression.

Michael **O'Dea**

Those Marches

When they play those marches
and the drums tip away,

I think of Brendan,
alone in his sitting room,
flicking channels,
news to news;
dinners collecting on the table.

When they play those marches
and the drums tip away,

I think of Peter
who hated cameras;
his reflection
in the mirror
between the bottles.

When they play those marches
and the drums tip away

I think of Tom
who asked for a present
on his death bed;
we didn't have one,
no one else came.

When they play those marches
and the drums tip away

I think of John
who asked me to visit,
the gentlest man
I've ever known;
I didn't.

When they play those marches,
when they play those marches,
when they play those marches,
the drums tip away.

Sinéad **Morrissey**

The Evil Key

In woods and lakes, car boots, freezers, huts,
the ministers' apartments where their flailing last

went on too long, garrotted, poisoned, hanged
or sliced in half and lain like Solomon's child

on the bridge of a border between two countries –
the myriad murdered dead of Scandinavia

are seeping their slow corrosion into the air, into
the tap water, and must be found. So many crimes

unsolved you'd think those dressed-down cops
in their open-plan offices balanced books

on their heads all day or practised on the sly
for the Eurovision Song Contest. But wait –

Denmark and Sweden's cleverest women
are on their way: obsessed, lonely, semi-autistic

and wired as no man with them ever is
to sense, without exactly evidence, where corpses

have been left: plastered into a crevice in a flat
in an affluent suburb or strung amongst the cables

of a lift-shaft in a disused meat-packing plant.
F# Minor, writes Johann Mattheson in 1713,

is abandoned, singular, misanthropic, and leads
to great distress. We cannot well accompany

the Devil in any other key. It will invert anything –
Jingle Bells, *Home on the Range*, Dick Van Dyke's

Chim Chim Cheree – turning them hopeless
and ironic, just as glass-walled houses

in the forest, immaculate kitchens, flat-pack rooms
sprung wide and nifty public transport systems

translate to mist in the brightly lit underground
hall of the coroner's workspace where three

blonde girls from the badminton squad
have hit their brutal terminus. We are given

less than a second
with their lacerated legs and hands.

Then cut to the churning sea with the moon on it –
the music making it worse – then nothing.

Matthew Sweeney

Into the Air

i.m. Seamus Heaney

I think I'll forget the concelebrated mass
around your coffin, the way those priests
claimed you as a starry one of their own,

and the high choral singing, meant to lead
you through the diamond-studded gates
of heaven, where you'd sign books for God.

I'll forget, too, the way that crow of a bishop
had to have the last word by croaking out
some blasted Latin hymn (although

you liked Latin) straight after your piper
played an unearthly slow air to guide your
coffin down into that hole in the ground in

Bellaghy, your own place, where, two
nights later a harpist was found playing to you
in the dark, as if you'd invited her there

to set everything right. I'll remember that,
and the piper's lament, and your Derry voice,
and your laugh, and yes, maybe a poem or two.

Country Songs

of all the emailed jokes and online detritus
that ebbed and flowed, in the autumn, between our
desktops
the best, we agreed, were the parodied country songs –
titles like 'How can I miss you if you won't go away?'
or 'If you won't leave me alone, I'll find someone else who
will...'

They come back to me now, in these small white days of
summer
and the joke is less funny, the audience reduced;
the theatre sits in silence – my phoney, lonely-heart
soundtrack:
'When you leave, walk out backward so I'll think you're
coming in.'
'If the phone doesn't ring, baby you'll know it's me...'

Dermot **Bolger**

The Piper Patsy Touhey plays in Cohen's Variety Show New York, 1905

Somewhere between the vaudeville skits and slapstick fare,
Amid the heat and grease-paint of Cohen's Irish Emporium,

When coarse laughter stops and catcalls quieten down,
I stare towards the dark pit that contains my countrymen,

And, stripping away jaunty tricks and frilly showmanship,
I play in the style of my father who died when I was ten,

Coughing blood in a tenement amid the maelstrom of Boston,
In a flat smaller than the cabin we left behind in Loughrea.

I've told stage-Irish jokes until punters can laugh no more,
I have used darting triplets to backstitch notes that soar

High in staccato pitch before lunging down towards hell,
Like those sea voyages in steerage amidst endless swells,

With no land yet in sight and a famished land left behind.
But now amid the growing silence as I stare into the pit,

I play this slow air for my father and for all my father's kind,
Who close their eyes and recognise their own grief within it.

Mary **Noonan**

Hi-Lili Hi-Lo

A song of love is a sad song
hi-lili hi-lili hi-lo-
but here we go travelling
the world, tracking ghosts
through forests, listening for birds,
for what their songs might tell us
of the one, the only – Hurry up! Hurry up!
This beast has fangs and will
gobble you! Let us go waltzing,
my love, where sticks are sharp
and shadows numberless, where
to look away is to lose your love
forever. Sing me a song of graves
opened again, of the dead lifted
into the arms of the living.
Take my hand, pull me down
to the wet ground where you are
rolling, hold me in your arms,
let me roar into the drains
for our lost children. Safety pins
will fall from the waist-bands
of old men, showering us
with spiky kisses. Let us sing
a song, our very own –
a song of love is a song of woe
don't ask me how I know.
Hi-lili hi-lili hi-lo-

Kathleen **McCracken**

A Minor

Once in a film
a blonde woman
caged in frames
saying 'every man has your voice'
and in your absence
I would hear
like the ghost of a crucifixion
your gold grain
russet tones
in the salt-inflected
invitations
of men whose names
escaped me
until I was not listening
to your voice anymore
but to its shorn undertones
bleached, scaled, bereft
of lights and edges
yet still alive somehow
the imprint of a resurrection
there inside this half-
hearted conversation
I am having
with my latest
metaphysician
when you walk back in from out of
snowfields
high desert
a floodlit landing strip
to ask the colour of the word
revenant
its syllables one intimate
long-drawn violet drawl
across the minor key of A.

Enda Wyley

Orpheus Speaks

Even in the catacombs I will be singing,
though my head has been severed, then hurled down the Hebrus
by those frenzied women, I will be heard still calling
your name, across the snows of Northern Tancus

or deep in freezing caverns. No wedding tune can move me.
I have made my own song, cried for you beside the Strymon river
yet knew there would be no music if you were beside me.
I could not have intrigued stones, oak trees, the curious tiger

if hell's three-headed dog had never growled
or Ixion tied to a cruel, burning wheel had ceased
to spin. If the ferryman had brought me back across the fen

that lay between us, you would not hear me now, roam
the black world of our separation, still singing in this tomb.
So, against warning I will turn, to lose you again and again.

IV

Girl in a Wheelchair Dancing

John F **Deane**

Canticle

Sometimes when you walk down to the red gate
hearing the scrape-music of your shoes across gravel,
a yellow moon will lift over the hill;
you swing the gate shut and lean on the topmost bar
as if something has been accomplished in the world;
a night wind mistles through the poplar leaves
and all the noise of the universe stills
to an oboe hum, the given note of a perfect
music; there is a vast sky wholly dedicated
to the stars and you know, with certainty,
that all the dead are out, up there, in one
holiday flotilla, and that they celebrate
the fact of a red gate and a yellow moon
that tunes their instruments with you to the symphony.

Dennis **O'Driscoll**

The Good Old Days

'The music of what happens', said great Fionn,
'that is the finest music in the world.'

The Fenian Cycle

And did his warriors not go on
to ask Fionn what the saddest music is?

I catch an old-style sing-song from
my Alzheimer neighbour's house.

She is home for Christmas,
her family have gathered in her name.

They chat about times past,
look back on her behalf to happy days.

Maybe Fionn's response was, 'The music
of yearning: that is the saddest music in the world.'

They press on with their reminiscing,
then launch into a further bygone number.

They do this in remembrance of her.

Macdara **Woods**

My Degas Words

for Eileene McLoughlin

Would you dance
for me
in an empty room

With tall windows
high ceilings
and a mantel-piece

Bare boards
A door
Onto a staircase

And nothing else
but silence
and the physicality

Of flight –
the weight of breaking
free and falling

Back again
As if suspended
In a mirror

The floating
rocketry and stamina
of centuries

Which I so want to see
up close
because it looks so easy

From afar
as all art does – except
for love

Which seldom can
survive
in time and distance

Without its own
delusions
its own constraints

Pat **Boran**

Master

Drummer with a country & western band,
he was master
of the standard dowel.

Like a martial artist his arm became
a rope of steel:
I am no style

and I am all styles. Breath.
Then that polished blur
across my fingers,

snare, high-hat, snare, high-hat,
tom-tom, timbal,
side, bass, kettle drum
                                        & cymbal.

Young Master

The community centre. Strolling past
on my way home from work one day, I hear
a body-tumbling-down-the-stairs
drum roll, then a cymbal crash.

Inside, alone on stage, a kid,
perched so high on a stool his feet
don't even reach the ground, sees
and promptly ignores me, steadying his kit

for a fresh assault. Time itself
is in a kind of trance: echoes
predict themselves, reflect themselves.
And, through the bars of light from the high, barred windows,

autumn reaches in to see
dust motes rise and swirl and bloom
as if something invisible had lifted them,
and held them now, nebulous, but free.

Mark **Granier**

Girl In A Wheelchair Dancing to U2

Lansdowne Stadium 1997

In a clearing near midfield
she is tossing her hair, waving her arms,

catching hold of, taking for a wild spin
a new constellation, The Chariot.

The centre holds. Big wheels rattle and hum.
Sparks fly from her.

James **Harpur**

Jubilate

We wish the chapel bell would just sod off.

But it takes it toll, coercing us to pews
of niggly nudges whispers wheezy coughs.

The masters come and turn us into stone
filing as slow as mourners, two by two,
as pious as Pardoners, in long black gowns.

The organist cuts his gothic horror chords.

Silence; mumbling rotes of prayers;
a psalm meanders; we fight to stitch up yawns
as the preacher scatters his pearls to swine.

Then Stanford's *Jubilate* shakes the air:

we sing like lions, a pride of one
primeval roar – five hundred gentlemen

like chanting Millwall skinheads at the Den.

By My Skin

for Terry McGaughey

Mr Bennet in *Pride and Prejudice – The Musical!*,
my father communicates with his family almost entirely
    through song.
From the orange linoleum and trumpet-sized wallpaper
    flowers
of the late 1970s, he steps with a roll of cotton,
a soft-shoe routine, and a pound of soft white paraffin.

He sings 'Oft in the Stilly Night' and 'Believe Me, If All
    Those Endearing Young Charms'.
He sings 'Edelweiss' and 'Cheek to Cheek' from *Top Hat*.
Disney animals are swaying along the formica sink-top
where he gets me into a lather. He greases behind my
    knees
and the folds of my elbows, he wraps me in swaddling
    clothes.

Then lifts me up with his famous high-shouldered shuffle
– 'Yes Sir, That's My Baby' – to the candlewick bunk.
The air is bright with a billion exfoliate flitters
as he changes track – one for his changeling child:
Hauld Up Your Head My Bonnie Wee Lass and Dinnae
    Look So Shy.

He sings 'Put Your Shoes On, Lucy (Don't You Know
    You're In The City)'.
He sings 'Boolavogue' and 'Can't Help Loving That Man
    of Mine'
and 'Lily The Pink' and 'The Woods of Gortnamona'.
He sings – the lights are fading – Slievenamon
And about the 'Boy Blue' (who awakens to 'angel song').

My father is Captain Von Trapp, Jean Valjean, Professor
    Henry Higgins –
gathering his repertoire, with the wheatgerm and
    cortisone,
like he's gathering up a dozen tribute roses.
Then, taking a bow, he lays these – just so – by my skin
which gets better and worse, and worse and better again.

Moya **Cannon**

'Songs last the longest...'

for Susan Hiller

my mother, who could not sing, told me.
As a young woman, she helped garner
the last grains of Tyrone Irish.
A teetotaller, her job
was to carry the whiskey bottle
which uncorked memory –
the old people remembered scraps of songs
when they remembered nothing else.

And today I heard a recorded lullaby
sung by a woman long dead,
in Kulkhassi, a language also dead.

No one understands the words
or knows what the singer might have sung
to an infant who may be a grandparent today
walking, haltingly, in the shade,
down a street in South Africa.

Did she sing about stars, or rain,
or tall grass, or blue flowers,
or small boats on a quick, brown river
or antelopes in a mountain valley
or a dark spirit who might snatch away
a little child.

Whatever promises or prayers
the song's words held
in that forever lost language
the mystery remains
that any infant on this hurried earth
could still understand the lullaby's intent.

Through its rhythms and syllables
love pours still
like milk
through a round sieve.

Paddy **Bushe**

Music Lesson, Xiahe

I remember it still, the young monk's delight
At the chance meeting with us on the hill,
The phrase-book hauled from the depths of his robe

Redolent of drawing-rooms and radiantly
Enthusiastic about self-improvement.
He opened it at random, and between

Introductions and *The Rules of Tennis*,
It offered, in English, Tibetan and Chinese,
The vocabulary of *Playing the Piano*.

You both pulled out imaginary stools
And, exquisitely occidental, he read
Would you be so kind as to turn the pages?

He tinkled and jangled the strange consonants
Around his tongue, applauding the right notes,
While *arpeggios* of giggles accompanied mistakes.

And as he fingered the unfamiliar keys,
The *basso profundo* of the huge monastery trumpets
Reverberated up the hill, and the great gong

On the roof-top brazenly imposed a silence
That would become the world's one note
In the fragrant, chanting halls below.

And to his *do you find the music pleasant?*
The phrase-book prompted you: *simply delightful!*
And it was. And it echoes. Still.

Emmanuel **Jakpa**

Tales

With the spliced rhythm
of tribal Africa, with the pulse
raw hide cloak of riddles,

with the drizzling monsoon
on lemon grass, with the serene river
songs of the canaries,

with the dim light of the oil
lamps, I reflect on the times when
under the tropical moon

fierce with shine like the sun
elders poured into the open palms of our mind
stories of tortoise, and of birds;

wise stories that last long in the memory,
like starch and Owo soup that's eaten in a clay pot
under a mango tree with fruit.

Vona **Groarke**

Music from Home

Six inches of weather, New Year's Eve.
I drain a tumbler of homespun
and plump up sentiment
like a goose down pillow.

The blue flame of the gas fire
sputters its notion of frost
as we count down
to the time-lag pip
of midnight's cheap champagne.

The lines are down.
The radio warns that secondary roads
are nigh impassable.

Come the tune and the first notes
of the opening year's slow air,

the blue lights of the melodeon stipple
two provinces, a river, slip of sea

and the fiddle in all its finery
leans into silver promises
it cannot hope to keep.

John **McAuliffe**

Continuity

The wind sails leaves around the house like late notices
of the garden's deterioration. Turn a blind eye.
RTÉ long wave announces gigs in familiar venues,
I like the presenter's comfortable thoughts of tonight
and the day after, until, that is, he introduces
The Holy Land by the Bothy Band and then
advertises a poetry broadsheet and a silver plaque,
before attacking quote the crimson tides
and purple mountains end quote someone (who?)
might waste his money on instead in Woolworth's.
There's a snatch of a shipping forecast and
I'm unloading the dishwasher when I hear a new voice,
which strands me by announcing, 'This is *The Archive Hour*.
And that was *The Long Note* 30 years ago today'
out of earshot as I am of the autumn sun and rain
which the radio forecasts, too, on this hour that's gone
south with its silver plaque, its piano and bodhrán,
where, in Woolworth's, a crimson tide progresses
beneath a purple mountain and someone hums a reel:
he knows the start of it but puts a question mark
against the title: it's 'The Holy Ground' but he doesn't join the dots.
He has places to go. There will be time again for names and dates,
for taking it all down, for credits, for footnotes.

Morning Radio

for John Scotney

The silence of the ether ...
What can be going on
In the art-deco liner?

Ah, now the measured pips,
A stealth of strings
Tickling the fretwork throat,

Woodwinds entering
Delicately, the clarinet
Ascending to a lark-like note.

Seven o'clock –
News-time, and the merciful
Voice of Tom Crowe

Explains with sorrow
That the world we know
Is coming to an end.

Even as he speaks
We can hear furniture
Creak and slide on the decks.

But first a brief recital
Of resonant names –
Mozart, Schubert, Brahms.

The sun shines,
And a new day begins
To the strains of a horn concerto.

Two Buck Tim from Timbuctoo

I found it in the granary under rubble
where the back gable caved in,
a 78 miraculously whole in a nest of smashed records,
as if it had been hatched by a surreal hen,
a pullet with a taste for the exotic.

I took it in and swabbed it down,
put it on the turntable and filled the cottage
with its scratchy din. Ghosts of the long dead
flocked from their narrow grooves beneath foreign soils
to foxtrot round my kitchen in the dusk.

I'd say Leitrim in the forties was every bit as depressed
as Leitrim is today, the young were heading off
in droves, the same rain fell all winter long.
Eventually one old woman was left looking at her hands
while the Bell Boys of Broadway played 'Two Buck Tim from
Timbuctoo',

and dreamt her daughters back about the place, the swing of
a skirt,
a face caught in lamplight, with every revolution of the disc.
This winter I have grown unduly broody. As I go
about my daily work an otherworldly mantra turns
within my head: Two Buck Tim from Timbuctoo,

Two Buck Tim from Timbuctoo. It keeps me up at night.
I roam about the rooms. I hope to catch them at it.
I want to rend the veil, step out onto their plane,
spiral down a rain-washed road, let some ghostly partner
take the lead, become at last another migrant soul.

The Rain Stick

Upend the rain stick and what happens next
Is a music that you never would have known
To listen for: In a cactus stalk

Downpour, sluice-rush, spillage and backwash
Come flowing through. You stand there like a pipe
Being played by water, you shake it again lightly

And diminuendo runs through all its scales
Like a gutter stopping trickling. And now here comes
A sprinkle of drops out of the freshened leaves,

Then subtle little wets off grass and daisies;
Then glitter-drizzle, almost breaths of air.
Upend the stick again. What happens next

Is undiminished for having happened once,
Twice, ten, a thousand times before.
Who cares if all the music that transpires

Is the fall of grit or dry seeds through a cactus?
You are like a rich man entering heaven
Through the ear of a raindrop. Listen now again.

Jan **Wagner**

hippocampus

what remained wasn't the half-downed limoncello
of a moon above naples, nor the suite
with a view of the gulf – it was the in-between
light, the gurgling behind thick glass
walls in the marine institute, the seahorses

mirroring each other, the two little seahorses,
each in its armour as though made of glass,
who seemed to stand rather than to swim, each twin
as if it listened to the other or to a suite
by bach, like the f-holes in a violoncello.

trans. Eva Bourke

Julie **O'Callaghan**

Misty Island

Sei Shonagon's *Pillow Book* tells us
how the smell of pine torches
wafts through the air
and fills your carriage
when you're travelling through the dark
in a procession someplace.

Here on this island in the fog
I'll have to take her word – 'delightful' – for it.
As I read the part where she says
'is wafted through the air and pervades
the carriage in which one is travelling',
'Down by the Salley Gardens' starts playing on the radio.

Mary **O'Malley**

Tory

for Lillis Ó Laoire

We'll take off for Tory
In the ship of fools
With a mast half cut, spools
Of carnival bulbs, lit. Roary
Rory at the helm,
Your only man in a storm.

Tory has the mandate of song.
On a rock in the middle of the ocean
We'll mock dead Autumn
And sing through the worst
Winter can throw at us.
Put a sock in the laments.

Báidín Fheidhlimí
Will take us to Tory. We'll be sure
Of a welcome if we keep in tune.
There's a king and a lifeboat.
There's a dog that swims with a dolphin.
The Republic of Tory is what's left.

Ciaran **O'Driscoll**

Wasps in the Session

There's a wasp in the session, zig-zagging
among the dancing fiddle bows. I see
the hills of Clare from a window behind
the keyboard accompanist, who's annoyed
by the presence of the wasp. Neophytes sit
with instruments *en garde*, in expectation
of doing battle with a jig they've learned.
Nattering non-stop, another wasp
plonks himself in a chair reserved for players:
music has pressed his talk-button. Praise
in this culture is indirect, addressed
to the instrument – *That whistle is going well*
for you – or to the time and toil devoted
to the craft – *It's not today nor yesterday*
you took up the fiddle. A stout countryman
pauses on his way from the Gents and stares
at the lead fiddler as if staring could
yield up the point, the mystery of the music.
If the global economy collapses,
these tunes will still be played, wasps or no wasps.
A dozen or so digital recorders,
some of them so small they must have been
designed by Flann O'Brien's Third Policeman,
are planted near the session. The wasps have gone,
one through an open casement, one out the door.
Somebody calls for a song. The Clare Hills
are looking good: I see them in the window
as if for the first time. It's not today
nor yesterday they learned to play the light.

Kathleen McCracken

Corn and Cockcrow

How well do either one of us
remember the Meridian motel
on Highway 11, north to Nipissing?

A raggedy man with a crooked hand
gave me the key to number twelve.
You parked the pickup truck.

That was before the comet swung around.
Ontario on the cusp of March –
barbarian month too cold for snow.

No tv, no towels either.
Slow heat, a single shot glass
but you were singing

cowboy songs, *corridos*
until the neon hum cut out
and frost ate up the silence.

I woke to sun dogs and your hand
sweeping leaves across the hollow of my back
each glide and pass, each gone caress
telling of corn and cockcrow.

The Green Fields of Vietnam

for Mick Moloney

Eleanor Plunkett in Saigon
   Carolan walks with Ho Chi Minh

The flying harp
   The piper's call

A fiddle carries Sligo east

And all that we have suffered, known,
   all laughter, hunger, hope is here;
The rebel heart, the burning land
   are held in string and bow, in voice,
and hands – nimble, strong pour out the music,
   unpick time…

Music pours
   and gives us pipers' tunes:

   The woman at the river
   Amhrán Grá Vietnam
   The Butterfly at the Wake

In Tarmon, Hanoi, here
   Jig and reel, slow air –

Remembering the end of time,
   the end of war

The good dead in the green and blue,
   in hills, mountains, rivers

   Music pours

The future hovers on the threshold of the past

A man in exile dreams his country free
At the Mouth of Flowers Michael Collins falls
The poet rides on horseback through the night

We cross from north to south,
  west to east
borders blurred and note made new

A blackbird in the Mekong sings
  The Green Fields of America
  and
  Cuach an lundubh buí

The beautiful goldfinch in a Saigon garden sings
  Nightingale and Rose

Time stops
  The dancer steps
  and poised
We stand upon the edge

  strike the note
and soul rise up
          and dance

Theo **Dorgan**

Singer
#15

Back in the long before, I was enchanter
and arrogant with the gift. I could make stones
move, men made me famous for it with their talk,
muttered sorcerer

as I passed, silent retinue at my heels,
and I confess I liked it, the awe they felt
a kind of sustaining echo to my own,
cold air to anneal

hot blade of thought. Now I am found enchanted,
the song sings me & gives me pause. The god intends
this, such has been made known. Reborn in silence,
I have recanted

belief in my power, surrendered my one art
to itself. By sea, by cliff, by woods I walk,
tending the busy music of what happens,
entranced with my part.

Singer
#17

Down in the villages I know they hear me,
how could they not? These builders of terrace walls,
tenders of vine, crop and flock, charcoal makers –
diligent, busy

people. I admire them, keep myself apart
all the same, can feel kinship without
needing to be among kind. Mine is not a
solitary art,

that's what I mean to say, and if they can hear me
when I play, they hear it all. The hesitant
runs, blank starts, whole liquid runs, they hear it all –
I can let it be

and so can they. I am learning how to play
as a child would, by doing without forethought,
not careless and not yet unconscious, keeping
out of my own way

Basso Continuo

for Vedran Smailović

It begins with a summer concert, wine. Red wine
carmine on white linen, evening light. Schubert's
Quintet in C. One cellist knows the score by heart,
turns his head, sees concentric rings

pulse in every glass. That night he dreams: a field,
bright air, the absent smell of death. No flies,
no sign the earth has been disturbed. He knows,
yet does not know he knows, what lies below and why.

No movement but his bow, his elbow back and forth.
Hoarse words hauled up, grim adagio.
He sows a solemn beauty and moves on:
another field, another town, another country.

Around our only world and round again, concentric
rings lapping the shores of every human heart.

Peter **Fallon**

from ***Ballynahinch Postcards***

A piper conjured
Easter snows
out of the blossoms
of the sloes.

❖

I'd begun to think
the like of this
might never strike
again,
the dance of days
in their rightful place.

❖

And then,
when we wanted music,
there it was –
the rain.

Medbh **McGuckian**

Novena

The nightingale only sings for a few weeks
each spring, and in royal woods, unwithering,
not for provincials left in their provinces.

He would not call out his magicianhood
to our snowy orchard redolent of graves
or shrouded arrowy in the death-pangs
of the late roses.....

his sheathed spirit would not break free
into its winged state on long light musky
evenings of a common blue stained with fabled
raindrops to a spangled veil.

Mellow, distant, resigned, and mouthishly
fertile in unmeaning miracles, he uttered
black swanskin in the thin hours,
and tepid prayers embalmed by hope,
a bird-happy hope.

They were wonderful windows and stairs
of flamy air that spun me north again,
and held the oil-silk edge of my lips
to the fire as my life and in my life,

as a beginning of living, as a forever
and ever feeling.

But all sounds flinched together on horseback
when I sent my arm's warmth
into the red streaks of the stone
as a sort of dedication of the summer
or the distillation of two winters

following the softest conceivable
opening of his mitred mouth
like the short, slow flight of the kingfisher:

yet hearing the dead swell
of what he had actually poured forth,
his whole, stirred-up note, in that
torrent of letting-go.

Moya **Cannon**

Night Road in the Mountain

for the Berlin String Quintet

The great black hulks of the Bauges
rise so high
that, this midnight,
the plough's starry coulter
is sunk in them.

Earlier, in the small, crowded church,
in the upper valley,
five musicians played for us,
stood, bowed, then played on and on –
munificent as a mountain cascade in spring.

We do not know,
we do not understand
how five bows,
drawn across five sets of strings
by gifted, joyful hands, can trace
the back roads of our hearts,
which are rutted
with doubts and yearnings,
which are unpredictable
as this ever-swerving
mountain road
down which we now drive,
hugging the camber,

informed by rhythm
and cadence,
happy to live
between folded rock and stars.

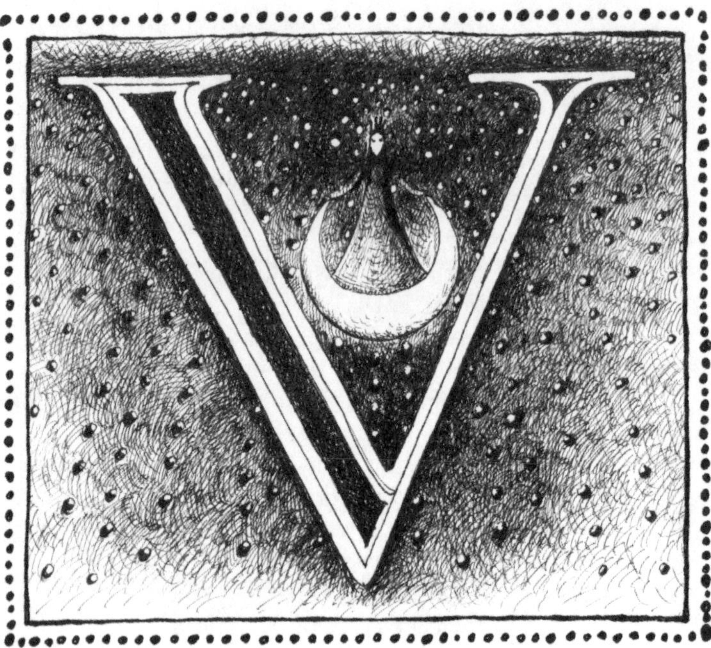

Three Men Standing at the Met

Michael Coady

THREE MEN STANDING AT THE MET

FRIDAY EVENING, NOVEMBER 4, AT 8 O'CLOCK

LA FORZA DEL DESTINO

(THE FORCE OF DESTINY)

OPERA IN FOUR ACTS (EIGHT SCENES)
(IN ITALIAN)
BOOK BY FRANCESCO MARIA PIAVE

MUSIC BY GIUSEPPE VERDI

MARQUIS OF CALATRAVA........LOUIS D'ANGELO
DONNA LEONORA........ROSA PONSELLE
DON CARLOS OF VARGAS........MARIO BASIOLA
DON ALVARO........GIOVANNI MARTINELLI
PREZIOSILLA........INA BOURSKAYA
THE ABBOT........EZIO PINZA
FATHER MELITONE........POMPILIO MALATESTA
CURRA........PHILINE FALCO *(debut)*
THE ALCADE........PAOLO ANANIAN
TRABUCO........GIORDANO PALTRINIERI
A SURGEON........VINCENZO RESCHIGLIAN

Incidental Dances by CORPS DE BALLET

CONDUCTOR........VINCENZO BELLEZZA

STAGE DIRECTOR........SAMUEL THEWMAN
CHORUS MASTER........GIULIO SETTI
STAGE MANAGER........ARMANDO AGNINI

Positively No Encores Allowed

New York City; Friday, November 4, 1927. That was then and this is now. Or maybe vice versa. Now is Saturday, March 16, 1996 and I'm tuning to a live broadcast of Verdi's *La Forza del Destino* from the Metropolitan Opera House. The music soars out of New York City to a satellite in space, overleaps an ocean, finds my study in a small town in an Irish river valley, animates the air between my bookshelves, earthing through my uncle Peter's battered old trombone which hangs in the corner. All in a moment of transmission-time from there to here. What has this to do with poetry? With the music of what happens? With some cosmic harmony of hearts? There are conspiring shades about me, standing again, listening to *La Forza del Destino* as they did on that November evening at the 'Old' Met in 1927. I have, spread before me as I listen, the printed programme which my future father sent back to impress his own father in Ireland. His written words upon the page which shows the seating plan: *This is where we stood.* His X which marks the place. *It is a passageway leading to the Orchestra seats.*

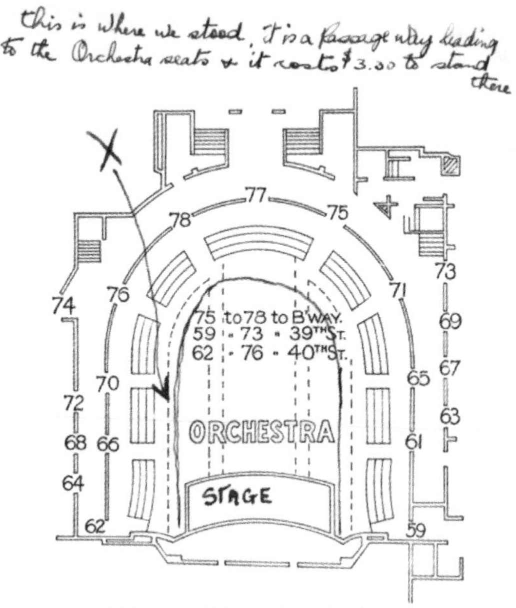

RED LIGHTS INDICATE EXITS

FIRE NOTICE—Look around NOW and choose the exit nearest to your seat. In case of fire, walk (not run) to that exit. Do not try to beat your neighbor to the street.

JOHN J. DORMAN, *Fire Commissioner*

My father George, his brothers Jimmy and Peter. Three ragged-arsed young immigrants, their futures yet unscored in an America careering towards the crash of '29, the great calamity yawning just ahead like an apocalyptic Niagara, its coming thunder still unheard above the roar of the Twenties. There they stand, these brothers, under the boxes of the Vanderbilts, the Astors, the Harrimans, the Julliards and J.P. Morgan, in a high temple of art and wealth and privilege, in a frantic metropolis of B-movie speakeasies, in a country soon to be flayed by a blizzard of collapsing stocks and bonds. *Ladies will kindly remove their hats during the performance. Reserved Carriages may use the 39th Street, 40th Street and Broadway entrances. The Buffet is located on the Grand Tier Floor.* In another part of the city on that November evening wasn't the young Duke Ellington raising a storm at The Cotton Club?

But those three young Irishmen know nothing yet of that nativity, that urgently American pulse and its mythologies. They're listening to Rosa Ponselle, to Ezio Pinza, to Giovanni Martinelli, to sounds they've never heard, words they don't need to understand. The plot is outlandish but the occasion magnificent. The music beats over them in passionate waves, as over me now, telling of relentless destiny, encounter, love and death, retribution and redemption. By day they casually work as house painters, sign writers, elevator operators. Sometimes on cold nights my father goes to the New York Public Library and transcribes poems of Yeats into a blank diary which, miraculously, will not be lost in time. Sometimes the three brothers skip work and spend a summer's day in Coney Island, touring the sideshows, gaping at the freaks, chasing the girls.

Jimmy, the eldest and the first to emigrate at the age of twenty in 1920, will never see Ireland again. He'll marry a girl named Leah Grimshaw in Long Island, of a family disapproving of Catholics and Irish Catholics particularly, though he will never again darken a church door once he's escaped the bitterly remembered clerics of his youth. He'll make his passion for grand opera his religion, scratching a living as a sign writer in Westhampton, accumulating a record collection of great voices, drinking most nights at The Patio. He will become outwardly assimilated but never content, watching as year by year the New York rich appropriate the foreshore, hardening into a bitter old age, in the end as unforgiving of his Long Island village as of the town he came from. Over the years letters from the homeland bring him word of clay on coffins: father and mother, sisters, a brother. Towards the end he'll write for photographs: The Old Bridge, Cooke

Lane, The Weir and Carrickbeg. Two years before he dies he'll almost make a visit back after fifty years. He'll get as far as JFK and then turn back, sending his American wife Leah instead. By the time I get to Long Island he will be ten years dead. I'll stand with Leah over the parched grass under which his ashes lie. Later his daughter will come to Ireland, find the green river valley, the town, the house where her father's story began. She'll tell how he first brought her up to New York and the Met when she was eleven, how he could never fathom her love of jazz, how he never spoke of Ireland. Had he buried and sealed it in some dumb hole he'd dug inside himself?

All this waits to happen as the curtain rises at the Met on that November evening in 1927. Peter, beside him, will weather the Depression for a while, then come back to Ireland to marry Kathy Healy, his hometown sweetheart ('the best-looking girl in Carrick') before some rival snatches her and in spite of the unbending disapproval of his mother, a hard woman of the Victorian shopkeeper class who is also a secret drinker. He'll rejoin the town's brass band under his father's baton and play the trombone which later I will play myself. The one which now hangs on my wall and sympathetically vibrates to Verdi. Later Peter will switch to trumpet in dance bands, becoming a noted crooner in pub and ballroom. Old sidemen still remember the passion he put into his best song:

Once I built a railroad, made it run,
Made it race against time;
Once I built a railroad, now it's done,
Brother, can you spare a dime?

When his teeth start to go Peter will lay aside the trumpet and take up alto sax, hitting the bottle hard until he dries out in his forties, then keeling over on stage at fifty-three just as he counted the band (my mother on piano) into *La Cumparsita* in the Ormond Hall of his hometown on St Stephen's night in 1958. The dancers sent home in shock, their money handed back as they exit. Buried in his musician's dress suit: he couldn't stand brown burial habits, not to mention churches, hospitals or funerals. Kathy, who bore him nine children, will live to be a handsome eighty-seven, with stories of his binges, the trumpet or the dress suit in the pawnshop, the throwing of crockery. All told with laughter in the end.

The third brother standing there will be my father. He's twenty-one. After he returns to Ireland he'll always wear his hat like George Raft and in drink say things like 'No dice, brother!'

He stands utterly entranced by Rosa Ponselle. A year before he dies in 1973 he'll write to her through the American Embassy, reminding her of how she sang Leonora in *La Forza del Destino* at the

Met in in 1927, his first year in America. The daughter of an Italian immigrant and originally a child singer in vaudeville, she had made her spectacular Metropolitan debut as Caruso's choice in *La Forza del Destino* in 1918. Her 'handsome stage figure and golden voice' were a sensation, 'with a seamless sound from rich low contralto to an effortless top C and electrifying trills'. In 1937 the Met's in-house politics denied her a part she coveted. She had a nervous breakdown and packed it in for good. Her secretary will reply from Villa Pace in Baltimore in 1972, when she is seventy-five and a year before my father will come home from the pub one night to face his final coronary just after he'd sung *There's a long, long trail a-winding into the land of my dreams*:

> My Dear Mr Coady,
>
> Miss Ponselle is recovering from a severe illness and has asked me to thank you for your touching letter. Your devotion to opera struck a responsive chord – especially remembering those unpleasant times during the Depression. Miss Ponselle has asked me to send you her very best wishes and to file your letter with her 'very special' ones. She regrets that this letter will not carry her signature due to her illness.

But that's still far upstream on that November evening at the Met. When the crash comes my future father will stand in breadlines until he finds a job assembling typewriters in the Underwood factory in Hartford, Connecticut. Dark mornings from a rooming-house, long lines of bent heads through twelve-hour working days, the ceaseless prowl of elevated supervisors' cradles moving above the production line. Outside the gates, turned-up collars and beaten faces waiting for vacancies. One night he'll cough awake to blood on his pillow. That dark seed he had carried in his lungs from Ireland; that intimate acquaintance which will take his father and young sisters.

In the tangle of chance and choice every effect in turn becomes a cause. When I am a boy he will remember all this by the fireside, in his cups. The Hartford doctor's advice: *Get back to Ireland young man*. The great storm on the passage home. His recovery under his mother's care. The dance he went to one night in The Foresters' Hall. The girl from Waterford playing the piano. Duke Ellington's 'Solitude' as they danced together. Their marriage and my own genesis, by circumstantial indirection out of blood on a pillow in Hartford, a place in which I'll find myself by chance in 1982, touring on an open Greyhound ticket when he's nine years dead. Remembering, I'll try to find the Underwood factory. Long gone of course, with Highway 84 inexorably rolling through its vanished assembly lines, its distant tramp of factory hands, its muted tyranny of time and hooters and long-dead overseers. I stand on the highway's margin, a tourist in sunshine pointing a camera at a factory which is no longer there.

A poem comes out of this: 'Assembling the Parts'. As the pen finds it on the page there is a jolt of recognition, the kind that's obvious once seen: within that mundane timetable word 'destination' the hooded arrest, the dark drum-roll of *destiny*.

In the long chain of consequence there are no absolute beginnings, no absolutely final endings. All things connect in time. Before she dies in 1994, an old nun in Carrick will invite me to the convent where she must vacate her music room and dispose of her treasures. She entered in 1926, the year my father went to America. Now, before she moves to a rest home after her stroke, she must offload her books, her sheet music, her bound Mozart sonatas, her old records. From the stack she hands me, all unknowing, an old Victor recording made on the 23rd January 1928: Rosa Ponselle and bass Ezio Pinza, with the orchestra and chorus of the Metropolitan Opera, singing 'La Vergine degli Angeli' from *La Forza del Destino*:

May the Virgin of the Angels
Within her mantle fold you
And all the holy angels
In their keeping ever hold you.

Dermot **Bolger**

Séamus Ennis in Drumcondra

for Tony MacMahon

I see him leave that flat we shared
And walk down Home Farm Road,
Black coat buttoned against the wind,
A countryman's hat pulled down,
And in his hand a battered case,
Containing the set of uilleann pipes
Found in fragments by his father
In a sack in a London pawnbrokers:
A jigsaw nobody else could piece together
A hundred years after they were crafted
By Coyne of Thomas Street in Dublin.

He carries his case like a secret dossier
That no passer-by could decode
As he boards a bus in to the city
Unnoticed among the evening throng.
Times are hard, our flat threadbare.
He survives on tins of steak and kidney pie,
On meals that he cooks at odd hours,
When he tells yarns and truly comes alive.
There is rent to pay, a meter to be fed,
Afternoon visits to the local launderette
Nights of wind rattling the rotting windows,
When he spreads his coat over his bed.

This is the price of making music,
Of living the life for which he was born,
He is on his way that night to perform
For little pay to a meagre audience
In the back room of a Dublin pub,
With a television blaring in the lounge.

Ignoring the jarring cash register,
Three dozen people sit, transfixed,
By a set of reels learned from his father
Interlaced with grace notes and tricks
Picked up from pipers who are ghosts,
Who died recorded only by himself,
Who never learnt music, wrote nothing down,
But carried tunes in their minds,
Knowing that with their own deaths
Dozens of nameless reels would also die.
Ennis plays with due respect for the dead
In his one good suit, a white shirt and tie.

Paul Durcan

My Mother's Secret

Like all women of her generation
My mother had a secret,
Which was that as a young woman
In Paris in the 1930s
She had played the oboe,
But that when she came home
On the eve of war and got married
She put away her oboe
And never played it again.
Only *she* had the key to the locked drawer
In the dressing table
In the marital bedroom.
Did she in her last years
In her show-stopping loneliness,
Distracted, disorientated,
At night in the mausoleum of her flat
In the red-brick apartment block,
Unlock the drawer,
Take out the silver oboe
from its satin couch
And put it to her lips
And, kiss of kisses,
Shock of shocks,
Horn of horns,
Blow on it?
Did Mrs Balbirnie in the next flat
Hear sounds in the night?
After she died
And her grown-up children
Had divided up
Her personal effects,
I trekked to the edge of the cliff
Above her childhood home
On the west coast of Europe
And holding out my two hands
I presented her silver oboe
As a parent presenting
A newborn baby
To the priest at the altar
Before letting go of it
To watch it plummet
Down into the opening-up beaks of the rocks.

Joan McBreen

On Hearing my Daughter Play 'The Swan'

My daughter plays Saint-Saëns. It is evening
and spring. Suddenly I am outside
a half-opened door. I am six years old
but I already know there's a kind
of music that can destroy.

My mother is playing a waltz, Chopin,
and everything is possible. There are lilacs
in a vase on the hall table, white among
the colourful umbrellas, folded,
full of the morning's light rain.

My sisters' voices are calling one another
far down the street. There are wind-blown leaves
under my father's feet as he enters the room.
I look at him as if for the first time
and he grows old.

I see my mother rise from the piano
and close it gently. She takes a glass
from the table. It is empty. But she has put
a weight in me, the weight of something
that has died in her.

As my daughter sustains the melody
with her right hand, the tumult
of the chords she uses with her left hand
brings into the room
the hush and roar of the sea.

Kathleen **McCracken**

How Old Is Ian Tyson?

You want to know how old is Ian Tyson
so I go to look it up, the way I'm always
double checking to be sure
and from the room next door to this one
I tell you he was born on September twenty fifth
nineteen and thirty three, how that makes him
six months to the day a younger man
than my father who died this spring and had
just turned the seventy seven Ian is about to be.

And I know you'll know what's meant
when I go off humming *Someday Soon*
that one he'd sometimes sing with Sylvia
about blue northern windstorms and the need
to make it up for all that's lost and gone.

Mary **Noonan**

But I Should Never Think of Spring

after Hoagy Carmichael

You brought a ghost with you, her prints
in the softening earth, her snowy breath
on the windowpane, on the mirrors, but mostly
clinging to the air between us, to our lips,
to the voice of Hoagy Carmichael as he sang
I Get Along Without You Very Well – you didn't
know his music but fell when you heard that, saying
you had never heard such a song, saying you wanted
to hear all his songs, your eyes full of soft rain dripping
from leaves, your voice full of sheltering in her arms –
I lay beside you and listened, looking into the dark eyes
of the fox, the dark eyes of the owl and Hoagy singing
It's not the pale moon that excites me that thrills
and delights me oh no it's just the nearness
of you, the nearness, you listening for a name,
or someone's laugh that is the same.

Leontia **Flynn**

The Yanks

It's 1944 and the Yank G.I.s
now stationed at the Ballykinlar camp
regard with open mirth my father's family.
The coins they toss them strolling past the house
my granny collects and makes the kids throw back.

The Yanks toss coins. The Flynn kids throw them back
but lend the soldiers flour-bags from the store.
They learn the Yankee pop-tunes on the wireless
but scratch a swastika on the store, and fly
the Eucharistic Congress Flag at victory.

Today my father has forgotten all the words
of those old pop-tunes he used to sing his babies,
their names as well – but The Yanks loom strangely large.
He squints his sky-blue eyes across the bay
to check on their movements: their strategies and losses.

Tom French

Like Cherry Flakes Falling

If I'd the knack
I'd sing like
cherry flakes falling.

Basho
trans. Lucien Stryk

The belfry of Saint Mary's across the Fair Green is closer to an aviary. In St. Mary's churchyard in Navan I have to stop to take in the voices of the birds. What I take for their joy, at the same hour every evening of these short days, is unbridled. I am listening to the incomparable Florence Foster Jenkins' *The Glory of the Human Voice,* accompanied by the wonderfully named Cosmé McMoon at the piano. As the Angel of Inspiration in the sleeve photo, Miss Jenkins is all wings and tinsel and tulle.

Finding, after a taxi-cab crash in 1943, that she could sing 'a higher F than ever before', Madame Jenkins had the driver sent a box of expensive cigars. On 25 October 1944 she braved a sold-out Carnegie Hall and died – of a rumoured broken heart – a month and a day later. High coloratura was her particular province. There is something deeply moving in someone who cannot sing singing for pure joy.

O singer, if thou canst not dream
leave this song unsung.

Things run. We might not have the technology to play the 60-minute BASF cassette boxed for nearly thirty years, which bears an inscription in Fr. Pat McCarr's meticulous architect's hand.

'Nationalism in Music' *(1982)*

The only surviving recording of your voice
is the school music project on a tape cassette
they shipped home with your personal effects.
My ghost *cognoscente*, my musical enthusiast,

I wanted to ask what difference music makes,
rewinding it for months to hear you pronounce
'Na-a-a-a-tionalism', and '*nineteen-tirty-tree*',
the great names – '*Borodin, Smetana, Mussorgsky.*'

I think I should have seen you in your cask,
touched your broken legs, your smashed wrists,
rested my palms on the bruise of your face.

When I play it now I play it to hear, more
than anything else, '*the music that springs*
directly from the earth, from no apparent source.'

If I played it now it would be to hear the accent of a young man who took his life in the Low Countries in nineteen-eighty-seven. It is useless to look for order. I hear my mother singing, '*Show me the way to go home. / I'm tired and I want to go to bed. / I had a little drink about an hour ago / and it went right to my head.*' Today Seamus Reilly and I are moving his father's collection of tenors on vinyl from the room built for it between the family home on Academy Street and the river. A lifetime's listening takes five trips.

At one point in the middle of the afternoon, Seamus sings, beautifully. All of the music in Ulysses is here, and everything that John McCormack ever put down on wax. (During the summer just past I heard on the radio that, when styluses couldn't be got in Ireland during the war, they used the thorn of the haw as a substitute, which shortened the life of the record but allowed the music to be heard).

I will return for the bespoke cabinets Seamus Snr. made, when his first born is gone back home to the United States. This is as moving a day as two men might spend together, at the service of the generation just gone. Seamus' father never took a drink in his life. This music was his thirst. These records are his ditch of bottles.

A Music Room
for Seamus Reilly

In a room built for music
by a man who knew how
a note was sung, and how
the plumb-line worked,

from which we have spent
the day moving the music,
reading labels, touching them,
there is one last thing to do –

find a socket for the player,
retrieve a record from the car,
slip it from its pristine sleeve
and bow our heads to listen,

as men who are praying bow,
to the static that brings us back,
then, out of the static, violins;
a man opens his heart, and sings.

The conversation, which hardly strays all day from music, puts me in mind of Ned Looby, the postman and music teacher who taught my brother and sisters accordion, and who cultivated vegetables in an allotment in the middle of the bog between Templetuohy and Johnstown. It's taken me this long to associate his allotment with his teaching, and to credit him with a talent for making things grow where everybody else dug for heat. 'Kevin Barry', 'Phoebe in Her Petticoats', 'Believe Me If All Those Endearing Young Charms' – the airs have almost all completely left me, but the drama of his arrival for the music lesson remains.

The Pillion Box
i.m. Ned Looby, music teacher

When I read
where they wrote
you had died,

I saw a fire lit,
our good room
occupied,

capitals stuck
to keys
to distinguish them,

your Honda 50
through our
Venetian blinds,

joined script
running lengthwise
down a grille

in Mother of Pearl,
a strap holding
the breath

of a *Paolo Soprani*
lifted
from its pillion box,

your gauntlets
folded, your helmet
stowed inside.

'*Now thank we all our God / with hearts, and hands, and voices.*' The music of the old prayers persists. '*Turn then, most gracious advocate, thine eyes of mercy towards us …*' Devotions …'. At the organ Peggy Gleeson leans into a hurricane of her own making. Fr. Bergin turns his back, dons the gold cloak and raises the great gold sun of the monstrance. A carillon of bells is shaken. Mrs. Cleere, in her turn, turns her back on God to conduct us in the gallery. '*Be thou my vision …*'. On the banks of the Owenduff, deafened by the noise of the river for days, this scene comes back to me. And later, for a friend who is putting down all that he knows about the Boyne from source to sea, I consult Fr. Dineen to find 'noise' and 'glory' meaning nigh on, where 'abhann' is concerned, the same thing.

Owenduff

'glór na habhann, the noise of the river'
Rev. Patrick S. Dineen, 1927

The silence I heard
on that last day
will stay with me,

when the fall
at the weir was met
by a rise of the sea,

and the uncommitted,
dry one who
waited for days

for the sun to swim,
believed all that
the ones, pausing

in midstream
from stroking to get
their bearings, said.

It dawns on me, passing back through St. Mary's churchyard, that those lines are the ones they might read over me. Looking up, I am reminded that the two-ton bell of Saint Mary's has not stirred in years, and hear again, my mother singing.

'No matter where I roam,
over land or sea or foam.
You can always hear me singing this song,
show me the way to go home.'

She came so far in darkness and in pain. The starlings in the belfry are deafening. It is a recording of the bell that sounds over the town's funerals and weddings and confirmations. In Saint Mary's churchyard I am lost for words.

John F **Deane**

Brief History of a Life

It is morning again in the old grey house.
Silence along the skirting-boards. Stillness

in the hall. First light. The boy-ghost
sits sullen, in pyjamas, top of the stairs,

fourteen steps down – where the carpet is frayed
and cobwebs frame the banisters; decades

down, metronome tock-tocks, and step, step, and step,
piano, the *Moonlight Sonata*, time! – faster soon:

Rondo a la Turka, allegro please – and now
that the walls and stairs have all dissolved, he still

sits, angry at the wet sheets, the dark, the unmanifested,
how the echoes of the 9th symphony's final chords

hang on the air before the thunder breaks.
And again it is morning in the old grey house...

James **Harpur**

Opera

Curtain up: the music master's car,
a backdrop of the silhouetted school;
blackout, then
                    a twinkling village,
suburbs of promiscuous orange lamps,
the West End's glitz, Covent Garden
          glowing like the Parthenon.

Scene change: Crush Bar hubbub
champagne chandeliers, silver-slippered women,
contralto laughter.
                              In seats of crimson
we watch mad Wozzeck stab his lover
and turn the starlit forest pond incarnadine
          by throwing in his bloody knife.

Lights off. When they come on once more
it's midnight, a wood near Shere;
the master stops and leads us up a hill
to gaze at the full moon:
                                   the whole of Surrey
unrolls in tops of trees, so still
          a song would reach the English Channel.

The final act: now back in school
we're creeping in the dorm; I lie in bed
and close my eyes and there, the moon again,
like a spotlight.
                         I bask and bow in the applause
that sweeps me off the stage beyond the world
          beyond the falling curtain.

Iggy McGovern

The Choir

from *Magdalen Sonnets*

Lusty May Day on the tower
And now, this glorious wall of sound
Barricading the mid-week cloister,
Mortarboards floating past the lodge.
I would have them sing a dirge
For Miss (not Missus) Gunne, marooned
In our church choirloft, the joys
Of twenty-odd pitch-challenged 'crows'
Belting out the *Tantum Ergo.*
Our Christmas treat a paper-poke
Of toffees known as *Danny Boys*
(jaw-breakers or her musical joke?)
The 'Derry Air then let them sing:
The organ pipes are caw-aw-ling!

Mark **Granier**

The Mock Leaving, 1973

What can they make of me, so studiously dreamy
I fall asleep in strict Bill Tector's class –
my ear tuned to nothing much at all

unless it's the *sotto voce* lullaby
from the desk behind: Rooney
intoning the same Pink Floyd lines

over and over: 'the lunatic / is on the grass...'

Michael **Longley**

Harmonica

A tommy drops his harmonica in No Man's Land.
My dad like old Anaximenes breathes in and out
Through the holes and reeds and find this melody.

Our souls are air. They hold us together. Listen.
A music-hall favourite lasts until the end of time.
My dad is playing it. His breath contains the world.

The wind is playing an orchestra of harmonicas.

Peter **Woods**

excerpt from ***The Living Note***

THE NIGHT BEORE THE FLEADH
EAMONN AND FRANCIE RUANE
with HUGH CAULFIELD

live in

DENNIHEY'S DRINK EMPORIUM

When we got to the door of the emporium we were refused entrance by a doorman I'd never seen there before. Caulfield shouldered past him. 'We're playing music here, you eejit,' he said, and inside he wasn't long evicting some poor man from his stool so Mary could have a seat. There was a crowd of Germans in the lounge playing 'The Morning Star', 'The Fisherman's Lilt' and 'The Drunken Landlady' in the settings they'd lifted from a Bothy Band recording, behind them a bodhrán rattling like calf nuts in a bucket. Frank Considine was driving the music in the bar from one of Cooley's tunes to another: 'The Wise Maid', 'Last Night's Fun', 'The Boys of the Lough' and 'Miss Monahan' – the musicians about him on all sorts of instruments: guitars, bouzoukis, mandolins, banjos, boxes, concertinas, bodhráns, bones and spoons. They'd drift in and out of the séisiún, picking up on the bits of tunes they knew, doing the round and getting lost as he drove into something beyond them. He put down the box and got up to join us and without him the music faltered – all heads were turned to him wondering what to play without him – its last focus stuttering like a tractor on a frosty morning.

Caulfield was explaining to Tull that he had no intention of paying for any drink and he was going to have his share of it. Around us the crowd heaved and swayed, pushing me left and right. 'Let's get this over with,' Francie said. They sat down and immediately went from tune to tune in an unending stream of playing. From 'The College Groves' and 'Toss the Feathers', 'The Hunter's Purse'; and 'The Drunken Tinker' to 'McFadden's Handsome Daughter and 'The Girl that Broke My Heart' and both 'The Copperplates', numbers one and two.

'He didn't get it from the ditches anyway,' Mary said to me. A piper sat in, assembled, buckled and launched into 'O'Connell's Welcome to Clare' and the music picked up more momentum, the notes from the two fiddles melting in with those from the chanter, the tattoo of a bodhrán, Considine's box punching rhythms through it and a banjo cresting waves on triplets. Outside there were faces pressed up against the window. People were banging on the locked doors to get in. Those inside were calling for tunes, yelping encouragement. You could hear them shouting:

'Give it the bow.'
'Skelp it out.'
'Play that one you played last night.'
'Play "The Bucks".'

The two of them were like a compression of air in that bar that night.

I played with them when we went back to the house. All our friends came back and people I didn't even know. They took turns at playing music, then the floor in the kitchen was cleared and the dancers rose sparks from the flags. It was the early hours of the morning; most of them had drifted off before I took up the fiddle. I was playing at my own tempo, odd bits of tunes, putting my own endings to them. Caulfield was trying to follow me on my meandering ways and Francie was laughing at him. Finally he gave in. 'Jasus,' I heard him say, 'it's like a dog taking a hare for a rabbit – not knowing its zig-zaggedy ways – he has his own scope, that man.'

I could feel the pungent vigour of alcohol dissolving in me and I felt loose again. I handed the Perry fiddle to

Caulfield and he held it, admiring the ripple of the grain through it. He contorted his torso in a semi-circle off the chair, sending the notes from the fiddle through the room, bouncing them off the stone flags and the kitchen walls. Then he handed it to Francie.

Notes flurried through the room. Tunes pitched upwards, igniting off each other. He improvised, linking bits and pieces of music together with his own joins – parts of tunes, nuances of tunes that were reflections of other tunes. I never heard anyone play with such inventiveness. His face was furrowed with concentration, sweat dripping off him onto the bridge of the fiddle. He seemed four or five notes ahead of the piece he was playing, as if he were waiting on the music to catch up, as if the music were a pure force of his imagination, to be carved from the air by the bow alone. He finished with a flourish, setting and re-setting the one tune, suggesting several different endings.

We played for ourselves that night. We played all the tunes we held in common, the music flowing together like liquid from different directions towards the one level. The first white light of morning was breaking over the lake outside before I bowed the first hesitant notes of that air again, exploding it into a slow run. The alcohol tasted sour in my mouth.

'Try this,' and Francie added a triplet, and before me, for the first time, that air came together, the notes quivering in the half-light. It was sombre music, like waking up to find the blood you'd dreamt of had seeped onto your pillow. I turned it again and again until Francie took up the bow and joined me for the final phrase. I laid down the fiddle and listened to him drag the air out into a hornpipe and slow it into a lament that seemed to settle over the countryside, beyond the open door, like a camphorous mist.

Rachel **McNicholl**

Breezie in the Organ Loft

i.m. *Lavinia 'Breezie' Sheridan (1888–1972)*

I often wonder how her feet
reached the pedal board below.
Perched aloft, she commanded the chorister,
Breeze, please – more breeze!
and the bellows wheezed while fugues floated
out of pipes and into the airy Pugin spaces
of St Michael's, Ballinasloe.

In her console mirror, 'Breezie' Sheridan
kept a quick eye on the priest, the congregation,
the Harry Clarke windows.
Between hymns, her mind strayed
to the Choral and Orchestral Society's *Mikado*,
to the Castlebar of her youth,
to Braga and Frankfurt-am-Main,
where she had taught young countesses music and English
before the Great War broke out.

While her fingers played familiar notes,
the Sunday roast
sat like a semibreve
on the horizon –
a few sherry quavers before,
a brandy rest after.

When I was a girl, this grand-aunt was the only woman I knew
who went to a pub on her own,
perhaps to pick up a naggin or two,
and I liked to picture her propped on a high stool
or sipping her tipple
in a tidy snug.

Long after she was dead and I had fallen in love with language,
I read that Lavinia, in London, had translated for the Service.
After 1918, in the Diocese of Clonfert,
Miss Sheridan was more Breezie and less Lavinia.

Tiny and stout, brusque at times
but mostly cheery, she taught generations of Garbally boys,
directed dozens of musicals,
conducted decades of choirs,
led thousands of hymns.
There was talk of naming a roundabout after her.

She lived alone – though not for want of suitors,
I am told – and there was clearly more to her
than met the eye.
No organ was too tall for her,
no loft too lofty.
I loved her kinetic energy and the jut of her chin.
She rests in Creagh under a treble clef.

Breezie was a multi-instrumentalist. My memories are mainly of her playing the piano at family gatherings, but there are archival accounts of concerts at which Breezie sang or played the violin or harp. Rowena Kilkelly, a member of the extended Sheridan family network, has been trawling the archives, and the material she has found gives a great socio-political flavour of the times.

To give just two examples: In 1911, Breezie sang the rallying song of the Gaelic League and later played the piano at a concert in aid of the Mayo County Infirmary (*Connaught Telegraph*, 4 February 1911). In 1914, she performed at a fundraiser in Castlebar for the local branch of the National Volunteers: "Miss Lavinia Sheridan, The Marsh, gave further proof of her claims to be an accomplished instrumentalist by the exquisite manner in which she rendered a charming violin solo." (*Connaught Telegraph*, 3 October 1914).

Her family, as far as the present generation knows, was moderately nationalist and would have supported Home Rule. Two of Breezie's brothers fought in the British army during the First World War. One of her cousins later fought with the IRA during the War of Independence.

Left to right: Joan Daly (my mother), Mary Daly, Mamie Daly (née Sheridan) and Breezie Sheridan at Rose Daly's wedding, 1945

The Faraways

Going to Connemara in the car with a father, a father who knows Irish songs. He likes to lilt. I lilt to myself, I mime a lilt. The scenery cosies all the way up to the birds' loft and the sky pulls the curtains. 'Peigín Leitir Móir' and 'An Poc ar Buile' could get an airing. The omens are good, any minute now the Teanga Eile might jump up and devour me. We drive into the relations' yard. The house is built on rock. We are beyond the place where road signs matter. This is not ring-a-rosary territory, this is read-a-face territory and read-the-eyes territory and read-the-oilskin-tablecloth.

The relations speak in tongues, full of sing, full of sorrow. The boulders watch every action and no action. A three-legged dogs brings luck, a four-legged dog brings a spring lamb, the sunshine a blessing, the birds a song. Dread is a creaking gate in a neighbour's yard or an upturned wheel barrow. Dread is difference. Dread is seeing the stars in the shape of a hunter. Dread is the black owl. Dread is an old woman's dream. Dread is a red-haired cailín on a boat.

I didn't know what a father was saying to the other two hand-clappers but they were laughing. They are going to give us boiled chicken and we better eat it quickly before the lingo devours it. It was a Sunday language without the holy water and a priest with foul breath and it had all afternoon for itself and us. The lilting was over for now. The sounds and the blissey-bliss was interwoven and it was tied up in an old dishcloth. I couldn't reach any of it but I loved all of it. Afraid was there, too, under a rock watching me. I'm a disturber.

Whoever she was, she was Boston-christened and they named her often. And they seemed to be able to see her because they kept looking out, the language rising and falling, the chicken dying to be eaten to spare them their loss. Every clock on the oilskin tablecloth told us what time 'The Faraways' got up and what time 'The Faraways' got the boat, but the oilskin tablecloth never said what time 'The Faraways' were coming home. That was that day and it went on for a week.

Another day, another Sunday, a father lilts: Di diddle di diddle diddle diddle diddle dum.
In the car with her father. We are in the tumble time, trees and houses are tumbling the wildcats. I want to cry but I mime a lilt instead. We are going to Connemara to visit his relations. A father stops lilting and starts singing 'Peigín Leitir Móir' and 'An Bhfaca Tú Mo Shéamuisín' and then he goes quiet. He is having sad thoughts. Then he snaps out of it and he starts lilting again. I'm still in the tumble-dryer. I want to vomit, but I don't want to spoil things for a father. I'm a disturber.

You have to remember where you came from so that you will know how to go back. Here you are beyond road signs, and directions are only for whooper swans and swallows.
A father lilts and follows the stone walls and reads the faces and the hands. The aunt and uncle come out to meet us again and they all burst into the language he loves and hates. The boulders watch every action, and no action ever staggers the boulders. They clock up every footfall, every blade of anxiety that surfaces when they start talking about 'The Faraways'. Sometimes they give the deaf ear, but they are just letting on. The boulders never sleep.

I want to go to the toilet. I ask a father and they all burst out laughing, "You see that mountain, a chailín? It's all yours." I am privileged to have such a toilet. I am privileged. A chailín likes the quietness.

After we eat the boiled chicken, they all look out. They look out a lot, same as the last visit. They are looking for 'The Faraways'. Where could they be? 'The Faraways' never come back to the place with no road signs. The other language is in full flight; they laugh and cry in it, and I know it's all about 'The Faraways'. 'The Faraways' did the devil's work by leaving.

This day a father decides that he is going to take me to see where his mother is buried. This is a treasure hunt. We get to the old graveyard and the boulders' uncles are spat out all over the place. I know that today there would be no 'Peigín Leitir Móir'. He can't find her. He tries this corner and that corner. She was buried just inside the wall. Which wall? I don't know one wall from the other. I mime a lilt. He tries all the corners. His face is red. She is gone with 'The Faraways'. But they went by boat. She went into the ground when a father was six months. There are no road signs or headstones, only broken ones or ones that slide down like a barrel in the bog. A father's mother is lost. We find no treasure. I feel sick. I am a disturber.

Back at the house the language a father loved and hated was getting a right battering. His father was a 'Faraway', but he came back once and had new boots and a suit for him. A father was happy. He thought: This is it, I'm outta here, good luck suckers, But a grandfather gave him to a farmer in Menlough to work his heart out until it was time for him to join the army. A grandfather told the boat to wait and he jumped on it and regained his status as a 'Faraway'. A father was below in Menlough, crying for a mother he never knew.

The treasure hunt ended badly. No sign of the mother who died when a father was six months. We were soon on the road with no signs. He didn't need directions. The stone walls were his map. The briars were his heather. His face was red. He didn't lilt. I didn't mime.

Gerard **Smyth**

from ***Dancing in the Attic***

In a Sixties dive, a Sixties turntable
was spinning the vinyl: the poet from Montreal
saluted the Sisters of Mercy, the troubadour
from Minnesota was pitying the Poor Emigrant.

To pass the boredom, girls were dancing wildly,
humming the chorus of a song from Merseyside.
It was a place to go on Saturday night to slake a thirst,
tie a love-knot or to find a consolation.

A Sixties dive, a house divided into rooms of homely
exile: dull surroundings of plywood and Formica
but beckoning with its blandishments –
German wine, home brew, apple cider.

Gerard **Smyth**

Ship in the Night

Falling from the ether, coming in on the tides
the Age of Aquarius arrived
with its pole star to the west
and California weather,
a time for the love-in, the street fight,
for the sorceries of the blues guitarist,
gentler strings for the broken-hearted.
The needle in the groove
scratched the tunes of a new troubadour.

In grandmother's halfway house
I was the boy who listened for hours
to radio broadcasts from a ship in the night.
A ship far from shore, with nowhere to go –
that hoisted a flag of convenience
above its cargo of songs in the morning,
songs in the moonlight,
the chanson of the chanteuse
who kindled desire in every man she knew –
my night-companion who sang me to sleep
with her blues that she blew
in on the tides and out of the ether.

Brian **Leyden**

excerpt from *Last Night's Dancing*

In a decade of free love I was constantly overcharged. Every film broadcast after nine o'clock at night on the television seemed to have at least one naked tumble, while on the home channel, Gay Byrne and the Late Late Show sent Irish bishops and self-appointed censors into tantrums of indignation for airing 'filth' during studio debates with vigorous audience participation and phone-ins where it was the cranks mostly who bothered to call – the liberals were too busy out having sex.

For as one old man said when asked by a television reporter what he thought about sex in Ireland: 'I think it's here to stay.'

There were few teenagers my own age around the village of Arigna, and no café or coffee shop. it was a long walk even to the grocer's. The nearest single screen cinema was fifteen miles away. And it was such a flea-pit it was said 'If you went in there a cripple you'd come out walking'.

Then comfort arrived unexpectedly in the form of sleek, lightweight transistor radios. 'Trannies', as they were called, were suddenly all the rage. They were portable, nifty and easy to tune between different stations. The old people could keep the big valve radio on the shelf in the kitchen with the aerial wire coming out of the back anchored to the upper branches of the elm tree at the front gate firmly fixed on Radio Eireann. But I had discovered the pirate ship broadcasts from Radio Caroline, and then Fabulous 208: Radio Luxemburg with DJs Bob Stewart, Paul Burnett, David Christian, Kid Jensen and the Powerplay. After Radio Luxemburg went off the air at night an American bible radio station came through on the same channel. I listened to the rich booming voice of a gospel preacher saying: 'I sleep good at night. You know why I sleep good at night? I sleep good at night because I have been saved.'

I hadn't found the Lord, I'd found Phil Lynott and Thin Lizzy singing about Captain Farrell, and head-banging bluesman Rory Gallagher 'Out on the Western Plain'. I'd found pop music and a breezy play-list of songs on the transistor radio that briefly and blessedly expressed the unspoken depths of yearning and abandonment stirred by a silent letter-box on Valentine's Day, or the up-tempo rush of summer holidays with school out for the summer.
I forgot my impossible crush on all three of *Charlie's Angels*, Jed Clampett's daughter in the *Beverly Hillbillies* and even the gorgeous Leslie-Anne Down from *Upstairs, Downstairs* got pushed from my number one spot when I discovered the petite, leather-clad rocker Suzie Quatro.
And late at night when the preacher came on air I raised my voice along with him and cried aloud: 'Hallelujah, brother. I have been saved.'
(...)

John **McAuliffe**

Effects

On my one visit to your bijou apartment –
Glass, wood, neutral tones – you went on
And on about important places you'd lived in,
Then hushed the room to listen
To a bitter night in wartime Berlin

When snow unmapped streets
Outside a hall bright with human heat
Where an orchestra played Mozart
And a choir sight-read sheets
That gave the text a fresh start,

'Hic in terra' for 'in Jerusalem',
'Deus in coelis' for 'Deus in Sion'.
Through the static, the boys' voices sound divine
And the crowd listen as if Requiem
Was made with their night in mind.

You refilled our glasses and whispered
In my ear. As the announcer declared
'That was. . .' you flicked on your CD,
'Epic Effects', first up a yowling Arctic wind
Rushed up my spine, then cold

Wincing rain, a thunderstorm that
Set me a-bristle like a catz
And your pièce de résistance, an at
Om bomb that I hear yet,
All jangle and unnatural collapse

With stringed seconds of nothing,
Then the whole bone china tea-cup asunder,
A swinging door creaking open.
What night could go further?
I said my piece, not that you'd hear anything,

And I walked home, in the rain and wind,
Wondering at what exact point
The day becomes night
In a landscape like that, like this, light
Disappearing from what's still left behind.

Jan Wagner

the études

forgive me, maestra, but i hated you
and your piano, the carpet-smoth-
ered wednesday afternoons, the row
of yellowing nag's teeth,

the instrument baring its keys, reluctant
to enter the house where the ivy's
musical score was let grow rampant
all over the drain pipes, the crown glass

inserts of the door appeared
to refract and pool the light, then blurred
as something large rose through the well-shaft
of the stairs and you, madame, surfaced,

peered down on me, impeccable and stern
as a fugue, relented and admitted me
who held the boogie woogie
for beginners under my arm.

how well i understand your short
temper today, the scales, the chords
long since died away – in a flash
it all returns to me whenever i chance

upon the ghost of your perfume,
heavy as a last act, in bus or supermarket
the tick-tick of the metronome,
merciless in its oaken casket

from which a thin cadaverous finger
emerged, the pendulum clock,
the photos on the wall behind the black-
lacquered monster; you heard something

inside it i could not understand, the two-four,
three-six time etudes, the shimmer-
ing lamp of tea on the table and i still am
not sure is it schubert or schumann.

trans. Eva Bourke

John **Montague**

The Family Piano

My cousin is smashing the piano,
He is standing over its entrails
swinging a hatchet in one hand
and a hammer handle in the other
like a plundering Viking warrior.

My cousin is smashing the piano
and a jumble, jangle of eighty-eight keys
and chords, of sharps and flats
clambers to clutch at the hatchet,
recoils, to strike at his knees

(*My cousin is smashing the piano!*)
like the imploring hands of refugees
or doomed passengers on the Titanic
singing 'Nearer My God to Thee'
as they vanish into lit, voiceless seas.

My cousin is smashing the piano
Grandfather installed in the parlour
to hoop his children together.
It came in a brake from Omagh
but now lists, splintered and riven.

My cousin is smashing the piano
where they gathered to sing in chorus
'My Bonnie Lies Over The Ocean'
beneath the fading family portraits
of Melbourne Tom, Brooklyn John.

My cousin is smashing the piano
where buxom Aunt Winifred played
old tunes from scrolled songbooks,
serenely pressing the pedals and singing
'Little Brown Jug', 'One Man Went To Mow',

or (*My cousin is smashing the piano*)
hammered out a jig, 'The Irish Washerwoman',
while our collie dog lifted its long nose
and howled to high heaven:
John Cage serenading Stockhausen!

Justin **Quinn**

Night Songs

I can sing few songs from memory, and I only learnt these for a particular reason. When my two children were young and would wake in the middle of the night, I had to get up and walk them back and forth across the room until they fell asleep again. Sometimes it would be quick, and I would collapse gratefully back into my own bed, but mostly it took anything from fifteen minutes to an hour. I had difficulty staying awake myself, and after a few minutes of hushing and rocking, my knees would bend inexorably, and I would tell myself I would just sit down for a second on the bed, the child resting on my chest. Of course it wasn't long before I was fast asleep. My child would sense the motor control ebbing from my body, and start screaming again. Wrestled back out once more from unconsciousness, I felt no love for anything in the waking universe.

So I decided to learn a few songs, both to keep awake and to add extra lull-factor to my pacing and rocking. I bought a book of old ballads (mainly Irish) with a CD in the back flap and set to beating out the rhythm and melody of "The Waxies' Dargle", "Scarborough Fair", "The Wild Colonial Boy", "Dick Darby" and even "The Wild Rover", among others.

I remembered "The Wild Colonial Boy" from my mother's singing, and that got me thinking in directions I hadn't bargained for. I began to wonder what was going through her head when I was a child. How did she see the world, or her life then, in the middle of the night with an ingrate baby that would not go to sleep? Who did she learn the song from? Was it from the house-help her family had when she was a child in Ballyhaunis? Or a Makem and Clancy record? What did she think about her own parents when she became a parent herself, pacing the dark in a house on Harold's Cross Road, with little sound coming from outside? In the past I had rarely considered my parents independent of their role of bringing me up, now I had long night hours, week after week to mull over the matter, all the while aware that I was printing similar memory circuits in the head – and heart – of the small human being in my arms.

"The Waxies' Dargle" made me think of Dublin pubs – mainly ones I never frequented when I lived in the city. The more I sang it, the more I marvelled at the witty elliptical way it dealt with hunger, prostitution and alcoholism, just as "Ring a Ring a Rosie" deals deftly with a lethal pandemic. Sometimes I wondered whether the subject matter was suitable for a six-month-old, but – hey – the child was going asleep, and I would soon be tipping, oh slowly tipping, his body back into the crib, most careful with the head, as a wrong move there could ruin everything. Throughout this manoeuvre, I'd be singing the song ever more softly, a kind of slow fade to accustom the baby to its gradual absence. What did his acoustic dreamscape look like at that moment, as the notes withdrew from the contours? Perhaps my voice was replaced by sweeter and purer voices, sylphs and seraphim. I've no illusions about my singing voice – anything would have been an improvement. And then again it wouldn't, as my child had only one father who could sing him these songs.

"Scarborough Fair" – such a beautiful old English song – made me think of the generations of people it had consoled, century after century back into the past, some of them perhaps rocking their babies also. It certainly didn't console them in a Victorian manner with the idea that love works out in the end, but its sad strains did make sweet a terrible loss. The names of the herbs themselves – repeated so many times – brought an imaginary fragrance to my head, and seemed like a pure good.

I would often forget whole stanzas (I've little ability to learn lines by heart), but I would improvise new rhymes while keeping the rhythm (sometimes I had to vamp a verse or two). Often these improvised stanzas would be weirdly unconnected with the preceding material; when I was more awake, I would force myself to keep the story line and characters. But the more I sang the songs, the more I realized how strange some of their stories were. The woman promises to be the man's wife as soon as he has bought her an acre of land – parsley, sage, rosemary, and thyme – between the salt water and the sea sand. You know she doesn't want the man, but the why is the music so sad? It's as though she's mourning the loss of the man even as she tells him to go to hell. Why do people ruin their lives like that? The song won't say, but it tells you clearly about the mess that people make for themselves. It also suggests that you, whoever's listening or singing, won't avoid this either, but at least you'll have this song to sing.

In the case of "Scarborough Fair" it seemed that many rivers flowed through its words and music – it was not the voice of one person. I wasn't thinking straight about all this, or consistently. It was all in small bits of realization, while pining for my own bed. But I wondered about the different marks that were left by different makers on the words and music. It often seemed as though a larger host of people spoke when I opened my mouth to lull my child to sleep. The songs seemed less like fixed, transcribed artefacts, and more like entities that flowed through time – indeed keeping time – changed whenever they were performed. I and the baby in my arms were just momentarily affixed to these beautiful patterns, before they dropped us and moved on elsewhere into the future.

When breathing out the music and words at such moments, I rarely felt close to another person expressing him or herself, even though the songs were usually about individuals. Rather it sounded more like the sound of generations – the children, the parents, the grandparents, the great- and all the greater stretching back into the past. This made me think about what I was doing in my own writing. Like many artists I had thought at the outset that I was expressing myself – my ideas and emotions – every time I wrote a poem. After this nocturnal experience with balladry, I began to think that the language just uses us for a while, before moving on elsewhere. Then you can go to sleep.

Derek **Mahon**

Rock Music

The ocean glittered quietly in the moonlight
While heavy metal rocked the discotheques;
Space-age Hondas gurgled half the night,
Fired by the prospect of fortuitous sex.
I sat late at the window, blind with rage,
And listened to the tumult down below,
Trying to concentrate on the printed page
As if such obsolete bumph could save us now.

(Frank Ifield, Clodagh Rodgers, where are you now?
Every night by the window here I sit.
Sandie and Bobby, I still remember you –
As for the Arcadia, though I remember it,
It no longer remembers the uncouth Coke-heads
Who trembled here in nineteen fifty-six
In ice-cream parlours and amusement arcades;
Oddities all, we knew none of the tricks.

Cinema organ, easy listening, swing, doowop, bebop,
Sedate me with your subliminal sublime
And give me that old trashy fifties pop,
Suburban burblings of an earlier time;
The boogie bins bouncing in rotary light,
Give me my toxic shame, mean woman blues,
That old self-pity where, lonesome tonight,
I sit here snarling in my blue suede shoes.)

Next morning, wandering on the strand, I heard
Left-over echoes of the night before
Dwindle to echoes, and a single bird
Drown with a whistle that residual roar.
Rock music started up on every side –
Whisper of algae, click of stone on stone,
A thousand limpets left by the ebb tide
Unanimous in their silent inquisition.

Eiléan Ní Chuilleanáin

The Percussion Version

Music is why we live inside
these foursquare rooms, why we gather
to listen to the scrabbling and the sound-test,
the way the splash cymbal explores the limits,
vibrating against the glass, and the bell note
rings and rises like a cloud into the ceiling.

From outside the house how different: I paused
beside the door and all I could hear
was a chair scraping into silence
and presently a soft step climbing,

a sigh from the upper floor, at which
in the room below something knocked just once
and the well in the back yard answered
with a bass vibrating groan.

Medbh **McGuckian**

Blue Kasina

I

You walk as if you are kissing the earth,
(She is breathing – why not me?)
Or tapping a page like a drum, you invite
The bell of my hardly used breasts to sound.

My second breast imbibes your graces,
The mind-river of my very first love,
Which lets the leaves pass through
As when he wanted my face to be more stricken.

You march your breastless body
Back and forth with all its volumes
Like a frontier, still agitated
By piety, blood beneath your everyday verdure:

As the semi-divine womb is able
To move around in search of moisture,
And will find it in an opening between two arms,
A path slit as if for letters.

II

I am sight-singing you, music
Made out of music, listening to the unfamiliar
Mass of your male womb and robust hymen,
Your someoneness, paid not to undress.

I am just this much inside your breath
All by itself where you die into
The tide of each unique breath
As the full language watering your mouth

With flow lines of water, their colourlessness
Almost intense. The drop of my dress
Into the pool of my dress is a brown garland,
A fresh crown, that has never been so closed before.

And for seventeen minutes I brighten
By watching like rarely observable
Star sets how your thoughts end,
Greeting your rust in whatever rings and shines.

III

The glassed subconscious of the city
Is overwhelmingly sweetened, the narrowness
Of the light is false, the shadow false,
Draping the window-cushions with gold watches.

So now each soldier has swallowed a draught
Of eau-de-vie in which the flag's
Ashes have been dissolved, we can
Begin again with the 'A' names

In the wood-book, using the soot of wood.
It is a kind of confusion of faithfulness,
This unkind holding of the torch of wishlessness,
That turns gently within my unmet gaze

An after key not turned far enough
To snag and soften all about it
The regrowth on the cleared table
Whose threading would give mile by mile.

Catherine Phil **MacCarthy**

from *Land League Cottage*

i Nocturne

I often woke in storm-black nights to find
him gone or working on legal papers –

changes drafted for negotiations,
his face by lamplight ghostly at table,

trim beard and brown eyes luminous
in solitary gloom, checking the words

he wrote, back to himself, each nuance.
It seemed then we were strangers anew,

his life, ransom for our bankrupt country
if late evictions are gridiron to go by,

and I lifted the lid of my piano
to sound the worn ivory keys and sing –

Love's Old Sweet Song – to lull my dear,
and draw him home again inside my body.

iii Orfeo

The lodge became a peaceful cradle,
the icy clip of horseshoes down the road,

a child muttered in deepest sleep,
the sea's low murmur. No light anywhere.

Or knowing when – days, weeks – he'd come
rushing to sweep each bairn into his arm,

waving a new libretto to tease me.
Alone, I lay homesick, the Oakland house

so far away, my old bedroom. How notes
used ripple from my breast – Che faro

senza Euridice – the orchestra leading
the melody, our town hall full. Now all

goes on without me. I hum in darkness.
Mama widowed. How I long to see her.

Letters take a month – bring news of friends
from choir – concerts, weddings, gossip.

VI

Listening
to
Bach

Kerry **Hardie**

Musician

for Maya Homburger

There's something in the presence, in the carriage,
a dignity that makes the player disappear,
as though a lamp's been trimmed and lit and lifted,
a clear glass funnel placed around the flame –

The sound runs through the body, driving clear,
so that I fly upon those sweet, high tones,
sounds that belong – not here – but somewhere else,
some other level that we partly dwell on,

as though the listening is given from there,
and we are being bowed like violins,
and when it's done, exhausted, we fall back
into the dailiness that lets us have our home.

Harry **Clifton**

To the Korean Composer Song-On Cho

Tell me please, what all this means to you –
Thirteen years in the west, the German night
Trembling the windows of your studio
As haulage thunders past, and the Hohenzollern Ring
Adazzle with traffic, the roar of Cologne,
Sex cinemas and drugstores, supermarket lights,
Dwindle, inside you, to a Buddhist drone.
Lay it all out between us, like the tea you bring

On a china service. Bass clefs, ideograms
Litter the floor-space. Peremptory, inquisitive,
Leaping from chair to chair,
Inspecting titles 'Clock, Toy Soldier and Drum
For the Leipzig Ensemble…' hardly believing my ears
At static buzz in the room,
Tinnitus, or the music of the spheres,
I ask you – is this how an Asian woman lives,

Alone, in our midst? Instead of explanations
Listen, you bid me 'The Stronger, the Weaker Brother'
Confucian, scored for the voice
Of an ancient woman. *Once, a bird flew south,*
Returned in the Spring, two pumpkin seeds in its mouth,
For the stronger loss, for the weaker one increase –
But please, no moral! 'East and West…'
You smile as you change the spools, and give the knob
  a twist,

Fast-forwarding us to the present century.
Silence. A drum. From the audience a cough,
Embarrassed, as it waits
And hears itself, in the terrible void between notes.
I look at you, and you look back at me.
Is this how it has to sound when the line goes dead?
Drum-tap, processional shuffle
At the court of the last boy-king, long since beheaded.

Flip the switches, plunge us back into silence,
Real, contemporary. The tea goes cold
Between us, and I watch you, as night deepens,
Listening out, for the gangs on the stairs
Who crowd your lovemaking, damn you for your laughter,
Rifle your garbage, cut your electric wires
And send you hate-mail the morning after.
'Now I can only write for the pain threshold…'

You say, as if no-one is here. 'Subliminal sighs,
A water-drop, the tick of a clock,
Or screeching kilohertz – but nothing in between.'
In the corridor footsteps, detonating through the
  apartment block
Like an echo chamber, bring the fear to your eyes
Till they die away, and the noise of Cologne
Takes over again, the razzmatazz
In a sonic void, where each of us is alone.

Caitríona **O'Reilly**

The Swan Theme

It was what passes for life:
a wife, six daughters and a reputation,
the scribbled song of gnats

amongst tall grasses in the middle section,
that drowse that hangs upon the air.
And even so: an outsider.

That the vision, when it came,
should be of such a nature:
an interruption of swans.

Above the buffeting rhythm of their wings
I heard their voices singing to each other
and so the melody composed itself

in a ribbon of radiant shapes,
a gleaming notation upheld on the staves of the air.
Then they turned

and flew back into the sun
and were swallowed in its haze.
When it resumed, the theme was of a darkened kind

like the blackness underneath the leaves
in May, that is more than shadow.
I mislaid it down the feathered vortices of days,

in the terrible anxiety of words that failed to form
but left their ticking rhythms in my head.
I heard it in the water's stutter in the plughole,

in the staccato cries of the telephone, in the intervals
of the ambulance siren.
In the laughing voices of my daughters I heard it.

It is all that I can do to punctuate the silence
with questions, to gather my chords
as the insects gather sweetness, from many places.

To look out again from the light's interior,
from the heart of grace, may well be beyond me.
And will they return, the birds of my youth?

excerpt from *Last Night's Fun*

The first time I heard 'Last Night's Fun' (no, rather, the first time I knew it was 'Last Night's Fun' that I was listening to, for I must have heard it many times before without knowing its name, or knowing the tune itself, for that matter), was from a record of the accordion player, the late Joe Cooley. Entitled simply, Cooley, the album was produced in 1975 by the accordion-player Tony MacMahon, who adopted and adapted the Cooley style to make his own music.

The recording is done in mono, and has that lively, crackly, jumpy feel of the old 78s, the kind of noise anathematic to the CD generation – and here I remember reading a pronouncement of the maestro Karajan, heralding the new technology in whatever year it was, that before CD, 'everything was gaslight'; well, what's wrong with gaslight? For you can use your imagination, make figures out of shadow. And lo-fi has a beauty and a logic all of its own, which has something to do with the imperfectibility of listening or hearing, or of the act of recording itself. Where do you put the mikes? What are you looking for? In any session of music, no one will hear the same thing: it will depend on context, on placement, on experience – whether or not you've heard the music before, whether or not the person next to you knows the tune that you might only half-know.

But do we ever fully know a tune, or only versions of it, temporary delineations of the possible? The boy sitting at the end of a row of five or six musicians will not perceive the tune the same as someone at the other end. Bar acoustics are peculiar. Wooden floors resound and carpets muffle. One hot-water geyser, unbeknownst to itself, will mimic the tenor drone of a barely-tuned set of pipes. The rhythmic rattling of loose change in punters' trouser-pockets has lost its plangency since decimal coinage came in. And the sound of an accordion played by someone with his coat on is different when that same someone takes off his coat.

So back to Cooley. As Tony MacMahon describes it:

> November 29, 1971, was a wet dreary Thursday, but Lahiff's bar in the village of Peterswell was thronged. Gathered from the nooks and corners of counties Clare and Galway were old friends of Cooley – people who had followed the wild call of his music through many a night down the years. They felt in their hearts that this was to be the last great blast of ceol with Joe.... In an atmosphere charged with excitement, and the sorrow just under the surface, Cooley played for his friends, while those who couldn't get in pressed their faces to the dripping November window panes. His brother Jack played the bodhrán with him, and Des Mulkere the banjo.

What follows, on Side One, is one of the best recordings of Irish traditional music ever made. The accordion is – as is its wont – slightly out of tune in the top register; and Des Mulkere's banjo is maybe not perfect either, and the bodhrán.... Box, banjo, bodhrán, an unlikely combination: it doesn't matter. The plectral, gunky sound of the banjo is just right for the business in hand. The supporting drum waves in the beat and off-beat; what matters is the melody, the beat; Joe's drawing out the wild notes in places, making little deft chromatic runs in others – bits and bytes and phrases constantly negotiated and re-arranged in what MacMahon calls 'the forceful logic which always seemed to run through his music'. And the place is jumping: whoops and gulders, clicking bottles, tapping feet.

The whole room pulses like a diaphragm, and you can almost see the punters hunched in gleeful shapes at the bar, nodding joyfully into their pints; for though this is mono, you can hear or see in stereo, as if you were some fly-on-the-wall, disembodied lucid dreamer, some ghost from the future, floating in on the sound waves that connect the present here-and-now to the present then, some twenty years ago. And in the lull between tunes, a few poignant bits of talk from Joe. The voice is grainy, smoky, hesitant:

> 'It's the only music that brings people to their senses, I think...'
> 'America is a very big place... but I think I was in most towns in it, anyway...
> Philadelphia, Chicago I was...'

and

> 'A lot of people all over Ireland thought I was dead...a couple of times...but...so...
> my voice is not as good as it used to be...'

Then Side Two, which brings us further back in time, to 1963, where Joe meets up with Joe Leary, the fiddle-player. He and Leary travelled Clare and Galway in the early Fifties, 'travelling dusty, icy or rainy roads on a motorcycle, the fiddle slung over Cooley's back, the accordion tied to the fuel tank'. The broadcaster Ciarán MacMathúna has gathered them together in the piano-player Bridie Lafferty's front room in Home Farm Road in Dublin. They play 'The Skylark', 'Roaring Mary' and 'My Love is in America'. Then further back again, we are in Chicago, 1962. Joe is playing with a ceili band. Again, the place is jumping; Joe is in full flight on 'The Ships are Sailing', soaring above the cacophonous drums and the buzz and clatter of the dance floor. We catch a snippet of conversation just off-mike, or just-on, a girl's Galway accent going 'I haven't seen him dancing in years'. You have to put your ear to the speaker again and again, rewinding and pressing 'play' over and over just to get the fragment, this isolated phrase in time. Who was he? Who was she? And did he ever dance again?

So to the last tune, 'The Sailor on the Rock', played with Des Mulkere in July 1972 in Galway. 'When you play this track,' says Tony MacMahon, 'listen between the notes for the great heart that was in this man's music.' So you do, again and again, hearing something different every time, trying to remember what you heard the last time, trying to relive those moments, not knowing what you'll hear in the future.

Joe Cooley died of lung cancer on 21 December 1973.

I turn over the sleeve. The sleeve is Cooley's face and shoulders and the upper half of the box, the straps digging into his collar-bone, the Paolo Soprani radiator-grille Art Deco aluminium sound-plate-and-fingerboard on his right, the bellows on his left stretched in an elegant accordioned ridge. He has his jacket on. A floppy-collared shirt, a tie; a jaunty cigarette between his lips. It is a gaslight snap, blown up till all the grains show, till you are drawn in to reinvent the smile you imagine to be there behind the eyes in shadow, as you are drawn into the gas of the recording, of the mono LP hissing blackly and revolving in its shellacky crepuscular upon the turntable of an archaic Decca mahogany-veneered radiogram the size of a china cabinet, with its dog-sized speakers and dead mice inside them, after you foolishly abandoned them in the back room of the damp mouse-infested gardener's cottage that you left for where you live now. I'm back there now and Joe is playing 'Last Night's Fun.'

John F **Deane**

Death Lullaby

Gabriel Fauré

There is a worldly holiness to it, the piano, closed,
a corner of the parlour mirrored in the polished wood.

He sits a while, waiting; when he closes his eyes he hears
the music somewhere above the city, the roofs of Paris

catching a white light from the moon's pale watching.
To open the chapel doors of the instrument is to release

the spirit, that comes stirring when it will and will not tell
its source, nor destination. He writes it first at the piano:

heart to soul, to mind and fingertips, wishing to send it through
to the other side, notes to the loved and gone,

envying the one who has discovered, at last, all truth and beauty.
He remembers that coward school-child before the bullies,

the Croix de Guerre after the Commune. After war, after a death,
what has been mellifluous will grow sombre; how, after love's failure,

write of tenderness? and after Wagner, how write at all? Fauré
plays as if the ivories were silk, the ebonies sable, his

Kyrie a kiss, his *requiescat* peace, his *miserere* an embrace;
Pie Jesú, the spirit breathes, and then at last *in paradisum deducant te*

angeli, soul, *pianissimo*, acceptance almost, the after-silence
lingering long, something accomplished, something achieved.

Vincent **Woods**

McKenna's Tunes

The Pitman in the Mist
A Trip to Cobh
The Sanctuary Reel
The Long Island Set
Carry the Buttermilk Home

The tunes we'd make if only we had the ear, the turn, the heart, the road for home. Disconsolate of a sports day, no one asks you to play, and heading away up the mountain you meet one man who stops you, saves the hour, asks for a tune, what to play? The Collier's Reel, what better in this place where years and wheels of time on again the man as small as he once was big, strong, frail now, rock dust on the lung, remembers meeting McKenna on the road and asks him to play and o the glory of it, the birds alight in the bushes, singing to match the man, and music catches time, holds it frail as moth or gable bat, flings it back to life, tosses it up and away and when the shadows gather in the half-set ruins, flitted under oak and lintel fiddle flute and dancing feet shout down the echoed moon and new rose tune bursts into scent owl as white as pit is black and coal flies softly all is one all is tune all is silence all is nettle all is fossil stone

Deirdre **Cronin**

No Strings Attached

for Mick Moloney

I am the tune that you shake free
from Micho Russell's Laurel Tree
dark roots needle the Doolin sky and lace
bright leaves in Micho's head
spindle intricacies of key light shadow
across his mother's gorse-thatched home.
And Gussie plays! While he Leathers Away at the Wattle.
You like the look of it
the mannerly fit of it
all air and grace and utterly unassuming
a house that knows the Humours of Whiskey
and heather-flower meal for the yellow goat of Luogh.

Cottage squat in its bedding
its back well crouched for the job
                                        the entire Atlantic Ocean
                                        needing to be beaten back daily
                                        in time   in time   from its pounding
just below Annie Moloney's bedroom window.
I am the lore in a mother's Hag's Head fear
foaming beneath her music's ear,
the sea's cut – where the good air
lifts the tail on your note of uncertainty.
You tap the door three times
survey the woman's stonewall
consider your options.
Your Limerick Rake has an edge to it
yet an undercut as soft as Micho's skin.
Nothing to be done though
Moher's rock face notwithstanding
neither point   nor prise   nor fret
you let go   let go   let plectrum's tremolo
Float the Crowbar   close your eyes
finger your trust in tones

of mandolin-coloured wood as warm
as a Doonagore farmer's hand on a Rambling Pitchfork.
You're young and you know it: this near dead
pulsing beat of life but also
the nuance in the swing
the slides of possibility
and a great feel for why
the widow is not the slightest bit impressed
those back windows weren't made to be open
                    to God knows what coming in off the sea.
Glass is caulked in salt but wasn't Packie's keenest
cut-stone sound beautifully smoked all the same?
You Walk to the Devil and Shake Yourself
Scatter the Mud off your Peacock's Feather
that's it   the window's out
                              and a small bird sweets the air.
Now Micho may sprout wings of Blackberry Blossom
pillowing the dream real of his love down in Louisville
cycle his bicycle straight from Mass
to Shepherd's Bush
bone box buttons to link his old coat with a boy's radiance
back when he crossed Flanagan's wet field with Annie's
blessing
to learn the luminous warmth –
warm as Patrick's Cat that Ate the Candle.

No tea – no son of hers – no whistles wet.
Music in her mutterings though – words
skite across a dry kettle on a hob
water-beading small hostilities.
Steam's ghost plumes a bellowed curl
concertinaed quiver   hesitant sea-mist
not lost on you either
you curve a note around old echo of her grace

that coy pleat over one departing shoulder.
You'd have settled for soda bread and scowls
even one salt herring
foreshadowing
the smoked Mackerel & Avocado Salad
demanded by the music starved pilgrims
in Connor's pub on Fisherstreet
where in 1988
European tourists will storm the gate
in search of Kevin Griffin's
tenor banjo plunked to the core.
But then   in the way of it
Kevin blues the air instead with his memory
of Mrs Russell's
Bonaparte Retreat.
He's below in McGann's now
reeling the Bellharbour Tune.
I am the gift of her ambivalence
enough Lisdoonvarna notes left in the step of her leg
to linger around your dance.
You with the hair and the length of it
the border-free cadence
the rumours of a mini-skirted girlfriend
from Sweden – and your first banjo.
That was well and fine enough but then by cripes
out appeared your reel-to-reel tape recorder
fishing notions
out of her son's head
and down the silver whistle of his voice.
Liquid filters
          limestone spills
music porous   clean
as a bell above Liscannor's water spring.

David Wheatley

The Treasures of a Folklore Beyond Compare

As a child I would perch in the tree-house and dream of scaling the tower on the mysterious German's land behind the estate. As a teenager my one desire was to play the pipes like Johnny Doran. Now my music has been and gone and my palms fall useless against my thighs.

The town of Rathnew is an unremarkable town, with its Wimpy bar and plaster Madonna, but here rests Doran, king of the travelling pipers, one chanter's toss from the Wicklow bus and its godawful radio station.

Among the most important effects on the pipes is the contrast between C natural and C sharp, as featured in so many piping tunes, Doran's version of 'Rakish Paddy' for one. Consider how differently he does it on his two recordings of that track, working the regulators each time like a pack of hounds on the chanter's trail.

At the time, forty years on, John Kelly, who duets with Doran on 'Tarbolton' and 'The Fermoy Lasses', still kept shop on Capel Street, and kept his fiddle under the counter. His fiddler's brow: sloped, confidingly, over the counter, through the window, as I walked by.

Some pipers play open, some closed. Doran played open. I prefer closed, but prefer Doran's open to any good reasons why I might prefer closed.

One thinks of Robert Johnson.

Hoist that chanter off the knee for those low Ds and Es, let the fox bark all it wants!

Pipeless today, I look up as the bus passes the cemetery and wonder where I have buried my music.

Sometimes he plays C natural, sometimes C sharp.

How I dreamed, as a child, of the tower on the mysterious German's land behind the estate.

David **Wheatley**

White Nights

in homage to Webern

over
nighttime roofs
to-and-fro

oystercatchers'
circling song
where

white
dusk-dawns converging
fuse-vanish

vanish-fuse
converging dawn-dusks
white

where
song circling
oystercatchers'

fro-and-to
roofs nighttime
over

Cloisfead Ar Neamh

Über Sternen muss er wohnen (Schiller)

Bhí Beethoven ar an steiréo, an tigh
Tonnchreathach, líonreathach, gairdeach,
Agus mé ar tí dul ag bothántaíocht
Go dtí mo chomharsa. Níor mhúchas an ceol
Agus d'fhágas dóirse agus fuinneoga ar leathadh
Nuair a shiúlas amach faoi ghile oíche sheaca.
Gotha an stiúrthóra orm, bheannaíos
Go mórchúiseach le ceolfhoireann na réalt,
Sheolas an uile nóta chucu, agus shiúlas liom
Ag súil gur chualathas an ceol ar neamh.

I Shall Hear in Heaven

Über Sternen muss er wohnen (Schiller)

I had Beethoven on the stereo, the house
Wave-shaking, full-flowing, celebrating,
When I decided I would go rambling
To my neighbour. I left the music playing
And doors and windows wide open
When I walked out into the frosty starlight.
Throwing shapes like a conductor, I bowed
Ceremoniously to the orchestra of the stars,
Signalled every last note to them, and walked on,
Hoping for the music to be heard in Heaven.

Eva **Bourke**

Riddle Canon

for Leo Treitler

on his 1746 Leipzig portrait Bach playfully
held the sheet with the music
upside down –
***
he turned it by 180 degrees –
a page spiraled to the ground,
a page spiraled upwards
***
the echo of a canon, a fugue, a flight
beneath the longhaired willows
that were as bespangled in the spring sun
as the king with his Machiavelli eyes
and silver flute
***
as if Bach were running in his Leipzig boots
across the cobbled square, his footsteps
pursued by the echo of footsteps
running twice as fast
in the opposite direction
***
the trick was to let the notes wander
like ants on the edge
of a Moebius strip
travelling along and exchanging sides
without collision in a continuous
circular motion
***
like Ouroborus, the serpent
who symbolizes the soul of the world
the beginning and end of time
eating its own tail
***
the royal theme reappeared
a six-voice fugue *ricercar*
'in contrary motion'
in the crab canon,
then upside down and then
in a mirrored upside down crab canon
and so forth
***
music turned on its head
as in the Leipzig portrait –
reflected in a glass ball
rolling

Gerard **Hanberry**

Listening to Townes Van Zandt

The lights are out upstairs at Rosie's,
the honky piano-player has gone back east,

the poker table's silent, the barkeep's apron
hangs like a strangled chicken from its hook,

there's a whiff of kerosene on the dry breeze,
balls of brushwood roll through the empty streets.

That light up ahead could be the moon,
or a half-shot musician on his roof in the ditch.

Gerard **Hanberry**

The Rocker

I came to stay for a few days,
his old friend from college.
Some friend I turned out to be.

He was into poetry and meaningful music,
a blind man could see she was bored fit to freak.
I got the bus to town,

came straight back with
two bottles of wine,
a red candle and Thin Lizzy,

Vagabonds Of The Western World.
Lashed it onto the turntable,
we danced, he slept.

Some things are meant to happen.
All so long ago.
We have a grown up son in Australia.

Yes, imagine that.
We were going to call him Philip,
after Lynott, our patron saint.

Joseph **Woods**

House-Sitting to Chet Baker

Came down from the cool of the hills
to the full furnace of summer, house-sitting
in the city, an airy wooden interior, stone well
under the stairs and a rumour of recent industry.

The jazz café in the front room was closed
since the seventies. Tables pushed to one side
new uses for the counter and marks where the window
was reduced in the slow recovery from the commercial.

Miles of records remaindered to play, but it was Baker
the needle got stuck upon *The smoke from your cigarette
rises up through the air...the thrill is gone...let's get lost.*

I fed cats for rent, brewed coffee in the mornings
and helped myself to refills. Watched motes of dust
dance in disharmony, his lethargy drifting through
the window onto a street of wooden houses.

Thomas McCarthy

Listening to Lera Auerbach

I can't believe I'd want to write that the sun goes down
Over the Blasket Islands on a near perfect day in July,
But I need to place the places in my ear, to orientate
Myself between the Blasket Sound and Chelyabinsk,
To settle my line of sight as a century of Russian colours
Falls upon me on the high road that cuts Dunquin
In two, isolating that hallowed graveyard from the sea.
Her *Preludes* are like those jars of mountain honey and those
Flasks of apple jelly they sent from east of Odessa
To victims of a more Westerly reactor meltdown.
Here, notes are sheep, poems are spoons; and this July day
In County Kerry, now that I need to mention it again,
Is the largest picnic table ever for her *Prelude* to rest upon.

John **Sheahan**

Ronnie's Heaven

What's it like, Ronnie – your new life?
Is it the way the old masters painted it –
Floating on a damp cloud
In the company of winged creatures
Listening to non-stop harp music?

I could paint you in,
But not your expectations:
"Would somebody for Christ's sake
Get me down from here and show me
The fountain of champagne – I thought this
Was meant to be a celebration!"

I'll paint a different picture instead:
I see your spirit, freed at last
From earthly shackles,
Soaring to a new consciousness –
Communicating with Kavanagh
Without the encumbrance of words,
Without the embarrassment of being barred
From four Baggot Street pubs ...

All is clear now …
Ulysses simpler than the Lord's prayer,
Beckett no longer waiting for Godot,
And Joe Ó Broin sidling over
With an impish grin:
"How're ya, Ronnie, you brought me fame at last.
I heard Cliodhna and Phelim picked me poem
For the end of your mass,
But you needn't have hurried …

There's no closing time up here –
Just one continuous holy hour."
Now Deirdre comes into focus,
Bridging and healing a painful absence.

Unhindered by bodies,
Your spirits embrace and entwine
In a never-ending spiral of joy,

Leaving behind the three
Great imponderables that tortured you:
"What is life?"
"What is art?"
And "Where the fuck is Barney?"

Dermot **Healy**

Somerset Maugham on Bass with the Harp Jazz Band in Enniskillen

for Roddy

The other night I came across
Somerset Maugham
playing his heart out
on double-bass and mouth organ

along with Spencer Tracy on piano
and a few other dudes
in a version of 'Ain't Misbehavin'
in Enniskillen.

Somerset Maugham was huge and lived-in
and kept his eye on the bar;
Spencer on the other hand
kept time with his chin –

What a din! What a do!
Jazz in Orange Halls.
Jazz down The Falls where old pros turn
into old film stars,

then later, going home, I think of
this Somerset Maugham
lying down in his room
just before dawn

somewhere off the Crumlin Road
where old LPs line the walls.
He sleeps among the greats
and wakes hearing a tune

he fell asleep playing
in a small café
in the South of France, yes,
in Marseilles perhaps.

He is playing a tune for the cast of *Casablanca*
who just dropped in
on the off-chance.
He's away now with 'A kiss is just a kiss';

'A smile is just a smile',
he sings to the pimps.
Henry Fonda is on his feet.
Duke Ellington steps

out of the shadows
to applaud Maugham on mouth organ,
and the plane carrying the Glenn Miller Band
has not yet left the ground.

Shostakovich

The wind and its instruments were my secret teachers.
In Podolskaya Street I played piano for my mother
– note for note without a music sheet – while the wind
in the draughty flat kept up: tapping its fattened hand
against the glass, moaning through the stove, banging
a door repeatedly out on the landing –
the ghost in the machine of Beethoven's *Two Preludes*
Through All the Major Keys, that said they lied.

Later I stood in a wheat field and heard the wind make music
from everything it touched. The top notes were the husks:
fractious but nervous, giddy, little-voiced,
while underneath a strong strange melody pulsed
as though the grain was rigging, or a forest.

In all my praise and plainsong I wrote down
the sound of a man's boots from behind the mountain.

Pearse Hutchinson

Listening to Bach

Gottschalk,
said Driscoll,
why've you never finished that poem about angels?
Because,
said Gottschalk,
I was listening to Bach.

Acknowledgements

The editors and publisher gratefully acknowledge the following for kind permission to reprint copyright material.

Chris Agee: *The nightingales* and *Nine years*, by kind permission of the author.

Leland Bardwell: *Outside the Odeon, Camden Town* and *Insomnia*, from 'Them's Your Mammy's Pills', Dedalus 2015, by kind permission of the author and Dedalus Press.

Dermot Bolger: *The Piper Patsy Touhey Plays in Cohen's Variety Show, New York, 1905* and *Séamus Ennis in Drumcondra*, from 'That Which Is Suddenly Precious. New and Selected Poems', New Island 2015, by kind permission of the author and New Island Books.

Pat Boran: *Concert off Kensington High Street* and *Master* first appeared in 'The Unwound Clock' Dedalus Press 1990; Young Master first appeared in 'New and Selected Poems', Salt Publishing 2005/ Dedalus Press 2007; *Guitar*, from 'New and Selected Poems', Dedalus 2007, by kind permission of the author and Dedalus Press.

Eva Bourke: *Swallows*, from 'piano', Dedalus 2011, *The Irish Tenor Michael Kelly Recalls Mozart in Paris* and *Riddle Canon*, by kind permission of the author and Dedalus Press.

Ken Bruen: *To Have To Hold*, by kind permission of the author.

Paddy Bushe: *I Shall Hear in Heaven*, from 'To Ring in Silence: New and Selected Poems', Dedalus 2008. *Cloisfead ar Neamh* from 'Gile na Gile', Coiscéim, 2005. *Music Lesson, Xiahe*, from 'The Nitpicking of Cranes', Dedalus 2004, by kind permission of the author, Dedalus Press and Coiscéim.

Moya Cannon: *Song in Windsor, Ontario,* from 'Carrying the Songs', Carcanet 2007, *Night Road in the Mountains*, from 'Hands', Carcanet 2011, *Lament*, from 'Keats Lives' Carcanet 2015, by kind permission of the author and the Carcanet Press. *Songs last the longest*, by kind permission of the author.

Ciaran Carson: Excerpt pg. 3-5 from 'Last Night's Fun', Jonathan Cape 1996, by kind permission of the author.

Michael Coady: *Three Men Standing at the Met*, from 'All Souls', The Gallery Press 1998, by kind permission of the author and The Gallery Press.

Harry Clifton: *To the Korean Composer Song-On Cho*, from 'The Holding Centre: Selected Poems 1974-2004', Bloodaxe Books, by kind permission of the author and Bloodaxe Books.

Deirdre Cronin: *No Strings Attached*, originally broadcast on Sunday Miscellany, RTÉ Radio 1, by kind permission of the author.

Louis de Paor: *Rory* and *Didjeridu*, from 'Ag Greadadh Bas sa Reilig/ Clapping in the Cemetery', Cló Iar-Chonnacht 2005, by kind permission of the author and Cló Iar-Chonnacht.

John F Deane: *Canticle*, from 'Manhandling the Deity', Carcanet 2003, by kind permission of the author and Carcanet Press, *Brief History of a Life, The Upright Piano* and *Death Lullaby*, by kind permission of the author.

Annie Deppe: *The Throat Singers* from 'Sitting in the Sky', Summer Palace Press 2003, by kind permission of the author.

Ted Deppe: *The Funeral March of Adolf Wölfli*, first appeared in 'Green Mountain Review' and was reprinted by Harper's, published in 'The Wanderer King', Alice James Books 1996, reprinted in 'Cape Clear: New and Selected Poems', Salmon Poetry 2002, by kind permission of the author.

Theo Dorgan: *Singer #6*, *Singer #62*, *Singer #15* and *Singer #17*, by kind permission of the author.

Paul Durcan: *My Mother's Secret*, from 'The Laughter of Mothers', Harvill Secker 2008, by kind permission of the author. *In Memory the Miami Showband – Massacred 31 July 1975*, from 'A Snail In My Prime', Random House 2011, by kind permission of the author.

Martina Evans: *Burnfort, Las Vegas* and *Elvis is Dying*, from 'Burnfort, Las Vegas', Anvil Press 2015, by kind permission of the author.

Peter Fallon: *Sean Nós, from Ballynahinch Postcards* and *Home from Home*, by kind permission of the author.

Leontia Flynn: *By My Skin*, *The Yanks*, and *Country Songs*, from 'These Days', Jonathan Cape 2011, by kind permission of the author.

Tom French: *Like Cherry Flakes Falling*, by kind permission of the author.

Mark Granier: *Vulture Bone Flute*, from 'Haunt', Salmon Poetry 2015, *Girl in a Wheelchair Dancing to U2*, from 'Airborne', Salmon Poetry 2001, by kind permission of the author and Salmon Poetry, *The Mock Leaving*, by kind permission of the author.

Eamon Grennan: *Kate Singing*, from 'What Light There Is', The Gallery Press 1987, *Untitled*, from 'The Quick of It', The Gallery Press 2004, by kind permission of the author and The Gallery Press.

Vona Groarke: *Music from Home*, *Interval* and T*he Garden as Music and Silence*, from 'X', The Gallery Press 2014, by kind permission of the author and The Gallery Press.

Hugo Hamilton: Excerpt from: 'Disguise', Fourth Estate 2008, by kind permission of the author.

Gerard Hanberry: *Listenening to Townes Van Zandt*, *Lilter* and *Rocker*, from 'Something Like Lovers', Stonebridge Publications 2005, by kind permission of the author.

Kerry Hardie: *Leaf-Fall* and *Musician*, from 'The Zebra Stood in the Night', Bloodaxe Books 2014, by kind permission of the author and Bloodaxe Books.

James Harpur: *Opera* and *Jubilate*, from 'In Loco Parentis', by kind permission of the author.

Dermot Healy: *Litany of the Wagtail*, from 'What the Hammer', The Gallery Press 1998, *Somerset Maugham on Bass with the Harp Jazz Band in Enniskillen* from 'The Reed Bed', The Gallery Press 2001, by kind permission of Helen Healy and The Gallery Press.

Seamus Heaney: *Canopy*, from 'Human Chain', Faber & Faber 2012, *The Given Note*, from 'Door into the Dark', Faber & Faber 1969; *The Rain Stick*, from 'The Spirit Level', Faber & Faber 1996, by kind permission of the Estate of Seamus Heaney and Faber & Faber.

Rita Ann Higgins: *The Faraways*, from 'Hurting God', Salmon Poetry 2010, by kind permission of the author and Salmon Poetry. *She's Easy*, from 'Tongulish', Bloodaxe Books 2016, by kind permission of the author and Bloodaxe Books.

Pearse Hutchinson: *Ó Riada*, *Pibroch*, *A Findrum Blackbird* and *The Miracle of Bread and Fiddles*, from 'Collected Poems', The Gallery Press 2003. *Listening to Bach* from 'Listening to Bach', The Gallery Press 2014, by kind permission of the Estate of Pearse Hutchinson and The Gallery Press.

Emmanuel Jakpa: *Tales*, by kind permission of the author.

Thomas Kinsella: *Song of the Night – Philadelphia, Carraroe* from 'Selected Poems', Carcanet Press 2007, by kind permission of the author and Carcanet Press.

Brian Leyden: Excerpt from 'Last Night's Dancing', by kind permission of the author.

Michael Longley: *The Stairwell*, from 'The Stairwell', Cape Poetry 2014 by kind permission of the author. *Fleadh, Words for Jazz Perhaps, Madame Butterfly* and *Harmonica*, from 'Collected Poems', Cape Poetry 2007, by kind permission of the author and Cape Poetry.

Alice Lyons: *marram*, first published in 'The Bread Basket of Europe', Veer Books 2016, by kind permission of the author and Veer Books, London.

Catherine Phil MacCarthy: from 'Land League Cottage' *i Nocturne* and *iii Orfeo*, by kind permission of the author.

Derek Mahon: *Morning Radio* and *Rock Music,* from 'New Collected Poems', The Gallery Press 2011. *The Andean Flute*, from 'Collected Poems', The Gallery Press 1999, by kind permission of the author and The Gallery Press.

Hugh Maxton: *War and Music*, by kind permission of the author.

John McAuliffe: *At a Concert*, by kind permission of the author. *Effects*, from 'A Better Life', The Gallery Press 2002. *Continuity*, from 'Of All Places', The Gallery Press 2014, by kind permission of the author and The Gallery Press.

Joan McBreen: *On Hearing my Daughter Play the Swan*, from 'A Walled Garden In Moylough' Salmon Poetry 1995, by kind permission of the author and Salmon Poetry.

Thomas McCarthy: *Bel Canto*, *Listening to Lera Auerbach* and *Scriabin's Piano Sonata no. 2 in G sharp minor, Opus 19*, from 'Pandemonium', to be published by Carcanet Press, by kind permission of the author and Carcanet Press.

Kathleen McCracken: *A Minor*, *How Old Is Ian Tyson?* and *Corn and Cockcrow*, by kind permission of the author.

Iggy McGovern: *The Choir*, by kind permission of the author.

Medbh McGuckian: *Novena* from 'The Face of the Earth', The Gallery Press 2002 and *Blue Kasina*, from 'Had I a Thousand Lives', The Gallery Press 2003, by kind permission of the author and The Gallery Press.

Rachel McNicholl: *Breezie in the Organ Loft*, by kind permission of the author.

Paula Meehan: *Two Buck Tim from Timbuctoo*, first published in 'The Man Who Was Marked by Winter', The Gallery Press 1991. *Home* in 'Pillow Talk', The Gallery Press 1994. Both poems from 'Mysteries of the Home', Dedalus Press 2013, by kind permission of the author and Dedalus Press.

Geraldine Mitchell: *Basso Continuo*, (winner of the inaugural Trocaire Competition 2012, first published in Poetry Ireland Review), from 'Of Birds and Bones', Arlen House 2014. *Grief*, by kind permission of the author.

John Montague: *Hearth Song*, *Windharp*, *Lullaby* and *The Family Piano*, from 'New Collected Poems', The Gallery Press 2012, by kind permission of the author and The Gallery Press.

Sinéad Morrissey: *The Evil Key* and *Shostakovich*, from 'Parallax', Carcanet Press 2013, by kind permission of the author and Carcanet Press.

Pete Mullineaux: *A Piper Prepares*, from 'Session', Salmon Poetry 2011, by kind permission of the author and Salmon Poetry.

Mary Noonan: *The Fado House of Argentina Santos*, *But I Should Never Think of Spring* and *Hi-Lili Hi-Lo*, from 'The Fado House of Argentina Santos', Dedalus Press 2012, by kind permission of the author and Dedalus Press.

Eiléan Ní Chuilleanáin: *Hofstetter's Serenade*, by kind permission of the author. *The Percussion Version*, from 'The Boys of Bluehill', The Gallery Press 2015, by kind permission of the author and The Gallery Press.

Julie O'Callaghan: *Saturday Afternoon in Dublin* and *Misty Island*, from 'Tell Me This is Normal: New and Selected Poems, Bloodaxe Books 2008, by kind permission of the author.

Eugene O'Connell: *On the Pier* and *Letters from Africa*, from 'Letters from Africa', Bradshaw Books 2003. *Blind Faith* from 'Flying Blind', Southword Editions 2005, by kind permission of the author.

Michael O'Dea: *Those Marches* and *The Green Road*, from 'Turn Your Head', Dedalus Press 2003, by kind permission of the author.

Ciaran O'Driscoll: *Catch*, first published in 'Prairie Schooner' (USA), Winter 2011/2012. *Wasps in the Session*, first published in 'Riddle Fence' (Canada), Issue 11, Spring 2012, by kind permission of the author.

Dennis O'Driscoll: *Nocturne Op.2*, from 'Dear Life', Copper Canyon Press 2013; *The Good Old Days*, from 'Update. Poems 2011-2012', Anvil Poetry 2014, by kind permission of Julie O'Callaghan and Carcanet Press.

Mary O'Malley: *Footsteps*, part of a suite of poems commissioned by RTÉ for a Joe Heaney documentary, published in 'Where the Rocks Float' by Salmon Poetry, by kind permission of the author and Salmon Poetry. *Geography* and *Tory*, by kind permission of the author.

Caitríona O'Reilly: *The Swan Theme*, by kind permission of the author.

Leanne O'Sullivan: *In Your Sleep*, first published in the September issue of 'Poetry Magazine', 2015, by kind permission of the author.

Justin Quinn: *Night Sounds*, by kind permission of the author.

Maurice Riordan: *Faun Whistling at a Blackbird*, from 'The Water Stealer', Faber & Faber 2015, by kind permission of the author and Faber & Faber.

Gabriel Rosenstock: *Lean Out the Window* (James Joyce), *Tar go dtí an fhuinneog*, trans. Gabriel Rosenstock. *Young Gypsy Musician*, from a series 'Ekphrastic Haiku', by kind permission of the author.

Peter Sirr: *Three Poems*, by kind permission of the author.

Gerard Smyth: *Little Mysteries*, from *Dancing in the Attic* and *Ship in the Night*, from 'A Song of Elsewhere', Dedalus Press 2015, by kind permission of the author and Dedalus Press.

Matthew Sweeney: *The Canary*, *Do Wah Diddy Diddy Do* and *Into the Air*, from 'Inquisition Lane', Bloodaxe Books 2015, by kind permission of the author and Bloodaxe Books.

Colm Tóibín: From *Everything is Susceptible*, first published in 'Cornelia Parker' (Maria Balshaw, Colm Tóibín, Mary Griffiths), Whitworth Art Gallery, Manchester, 2015, by kind permission of the author.

Jan Wagner, trans. Eva Bourke: *hippocampus*, *giovanni gnocchi plays the cello* and *the études*, German originals published in 'regentonnenvariationen', Hanser Verlag, 2014, by kind permission of the author and Eva Bourke.

David Wheatley: *Klangfarbenmelodie*, first published in the 'Cincinnati Review', *The Treasures of a Folklore beyond Compare*, first published in 'The Wake Forest Series of Irish Poetry', Vol. 1 (Wake Forest University Press 2005), *White Nights* first published in 'The Weary Blues' (online). *Sonnets to Robert Fergusson* first published in 'The Evergreen', by kind permission of the author and Wake Forest University Press.

Joseph Woods: *House Sitting to Chet Baker* and *Singing Gate*, from 'Ballyowen', first published in 'Bearings', Worple Press 2005, reissued as 'Cargo', Dedalus Press 2010, by kind permission of the author and Dedalus Press.

Macdara Woods: *My Degas Words* and *Salt Fields*, from 'Music From the Big Tent', Dedalus Press 2016, by kind permission of the author and Dedalus Press.

Peter Woods: Excerpt from 'The Living Note: The Heartbeat of Irish Music' (Christy McNamara and Peter Woods), The O'Brien Press 1996, by kind permission of the author.

Vincent Woods: *The Green Fields of Vietnam*, first published in The Irish Times; *McKenna's Tunes* originally broadcast on Sunday Miscellany, RTÉ Radio 1, by kind permission of the author.

Enda Wyley: *Cúil Aodha Singer* and *Orpheus Speaks*, from 'New and Selected Poems', Dedalus Press 2014, by kind permission of the author and Dedalus Press.

Index

A

Agee, Chris
The nightingales 34 *Nine years* 99

B

Bardwell, Leland
Outside the Odeon, Camden Town 104 *Insomnia* 105

Bolger, Dermot
The Piper Patsy Touhey Plays in Cohen's Variety Show, New York, 1905 144
Séamus Ennis in Drumcondra 188

Boran, Pat
Concert off Kensington High Street 86 *Guitar* 92 *Master* 153
Young Master 153

Bourke, Eva
Swallows 45 *The Irish Tenor Michael Kelly Recalls Mozart in Paris* 122
Riddle Canon 249

See also Jan Wagner

Bruen, Ken
To Have To Hold 132

Bushe, Paddy
Music Lesson, Xiahe 158
I Shall Hear in Heaven 248 *Cloisfead ar Neamh* 248

C

Cannon, Moya
Song in Windsor, Ontario 43 *Lament* 116 *'Songs last the longest...'* 157
Night Road in the Mountain 177

Carson, Ciaran
Last Night's Fun excerpt 236

Coady, Michael
Three Men Standing at the Met 180

Clifton, Harry
To the Korean Composer Song-On Cho 233

Cronin, Deirdre
No Strings Attached 242

D

de Paor,Louis
Didjeridu 62 63 *Rory* 100 101

Deane, John F
The Upright Piano 57 *Canticle* 150 *Brief History of a Life* 199
Death Lullaby 240

de Ventadorn, Bernart, see **Sirr**, Peter

Deppe, Annie
The Throat Singers 64

Deppe, Ted
The Funeral March of Adolf Wölfli 124

Dorgan, Theo
Singer #6 68 *Singer #62* 69 *Singer #15* 172 *Singer #17* 173

Durcan, Paul
In Memory the Miami Showband – Massacred 31 July 1975 102
My Mother's Secret 189

E

Evans, Martina
Burnfort, Las Vegas 130 *Elvis is Dying* 131

F

Fallon, Peter
Home from Home 49 *Sean Nós* 67 from *Ballynahinch Postcards* 175

Flynn, Leontia
Country Songs 143 *By My Skin* 156 *The Yanks* 193

French, Tom
Like Cherry Flakes Falling 194

G

Granier, Mark
Vulture Bone Flute 58 *Girl in a Wheelchair Dancing to U2* 154
The Mock Leaving 202

Grennan, Eamon
Untitled 32 *Kate Singing* 60

Groarke, Vona
The Garden as Music and Silence 33 *Interval* 5
Music from Home 160

H

Hamilton, Hugo
Disguise excerpt 88

Hanberry, Gerard
Lilter 70 *Listening to Townes Van Zandt* 250 *Rocker* 251

Hardie, Kerry
Leaf-Fall 41 *Musician* 232

Harpur, James
Opera 200 *Jubilate* 155

Healy, Dermot
The Litany of the Wagtail 50
Somerset Maugham on Bass with the Harp Jazz Band in Enniskillen 256

Heaney, Seamus
The Canopy 31 *The Given Note* 56 *The Rain Stick* 164

Higgins, Rita Ann
She's Easy 66 *The Faraways* 211

Hutchinson, Pearse
A Findrum Blackbird 35 *Pibroch* 72 *The Miracle of Bread and Fiddles* 79
Ó Riada 103 *Listening to Bach* 259

J

Jakpa, Emmanuel
Tales 159

Joyce, James
Lean out of the window 80
Tar to dtí an fhuinneog (*trans. Gabriel Rosenstock*) 81

K

Kinsella, Thomas
Song of the Night – Philadelphia, Carraroe 36

L

Leyden, Brian
Last Night's Dancing excerpt 216

Longley, Michael
The Stairwell 30 *Fleadh* 74 *Words for Jazz Perhaps* 106
Madame Butterfly 120 *Harmonica* 203

Lyons, Alice
marram 46

M

MacCarthy, Catherine Phil
from *Land League Cottage i. Nocturne* 228 *iii Orfeo* 229

Mahon, Derek
The Andean Flute 77 *Morning Radio* 162 *Rock Music* 224

Maxton, Hugh
War and Music 109

McAuliffe, John
At a Concert 128 *Continuity* 161 *Effects* 218

McBreen, Joan
On Hearing my Daughter Play the Swan 190

McCarthy, Thomas
Bel Canto 76 *Scriabin's Piano Sonata No. 2 in G sharp minor, Opus 19* 121 *Listening to Lera Auerbach* 253

McCracken, Kathleen
A Minor 146 *Corn and Cockcrow* 169 *How Old Is Ian Tyson?* 191

McGovern, Iggy
The Choir 201

McGuckian, Medbh
Novena 176 *Blue Kasina* 226

McNicholl, Rachel
Breezie in the Organ Loft 208

Meehan, Paula
Home 110 *Two Buck Tim from Timbuctoo* 163

Mitchell, Geraldine
Grief 112 *Basso Continuo* 174

Montague, John
Hearth Song 28 *Windharp* 29 *Lullaby* 113
The Family Piano 220

Morrissey, Sinéad
The Evil Key 140 *Shostakovich* 258

Mullineaux, Pete
A Piper Prepares 95

N

Noonan, Mary
The Fado House of Argentina Santos 78 *Hi-Lili Hi-Lo* 145
But I Should Never Think of Spring 192

Ní Chuilleanáin, Eiléan
Hofstetter's Serenade 98 *The Percussion Version* 225

O

O'Callaghan, Julie
Saturday Afternoon in Dublin 127 *Misty Island* 166

O'Connell, Eugene
Blind Faith 93 *On the Pier* 126 *Letters from Africa* 126

O'Dea, Michael
The Green Road 44 *Those Marches* 139

O'Driscoll, Ciaran
Catch 71 *Wasps in the Session* 168

O'Driscoll, Dennis
Nocturne Op.2 115 *The Good Old Days* 151

O'Malley, Mary
Geography 39 *Footsteps* 73 *Tory* 167

O'Reilly, Caitríona
The Swan Theme 235

O'Sullivan, Leanne
In Your Sleep 114

Q

Quinn, Justin
Night Songs 221

R

Riordan, Maurice
Faun Whistling to a Blackbird 49

Rosenstock, Gabriel
Young Gypsy Musician 52

See also Joyce, James

S

Sheahan, John
Ronnie's Heaven 254

Sirr, Peter
Three Poems 82

Smyth, Gerard
Little Mysteries 90 from *Dancing in the Attic* 214 *Ship in the Night* 215

Sweeney, Matthew
The Canary 42 *Do Wah Diddy Diddy Do* 61 *Into the Air* 142

T

Tóibín, Colm
Everything is Susceptible excerpt 117

W

Wagner, Jan, trans. Eva Bourke
giovanni gnocchi plays the cello 87 *hippocampus* 165 *the études* 219

Wheatley, David
Klangfarbenmelodie 40 *Sonnets to Robert Fergusson* 129
The Treasures of a Folklore beyond Compare 246 *White Nights* 247

Woods, Joseph
Singing Gate 48 *House Sitting to Chet Baker* 252

Woods, Macdara
Salt Fields 108 *My Degas Words* 152

Woods, Peter
The Living Note extract 204

Woods, Vincent
The Green Fields of Vietnam 170 *McKenna's Tunes* 241

Wyley, Enda
Cúil Aodha Singer 91 *Orpheus Speaks* 147

Photography

Christy **McNamara**
Stone Wall 44 *Jim Carrigan, Piper* 94
Sisters Bridie Callinan and Kathleen O'Loughlin, Ruan, Co Clare 171
Wexford fiddler, Tom Dunne 206 *Micho Russell* 243

Eva **Besnyö** 53

Photograph of *Breezie Sheridan* 210, courtesy of Rachel McNicholl

Illustrations

Miriam **de Búrca**
Front and back cover, 26, 54, 96, 148, 178, 230

Eva **Bourke**

Eva Bourke is a poet and translator. She has published six collections of poetry, among them *Spring in Henry Street*, *Travels with Gandolpho*, *The Latitude of Naples* and most recently *piano* (Dedalus 2011) which among other things charts her lifelong passion for music. She has published several anthologies and collections of poetry in translation both in English and German, and together with Borbála Farragó she edited an anthology of immigrant poets to Ireland, entitled *Landing Places* (2010, Dedalus Press). Her work has been widely translated and she has taught and lectured in MFA programmes at universities in the USA and Ireland, has received numerous awards and bursaries. She lives in Galway and Berlin and is a member of Aosdána.

Vincent **Woods**

Vincent Woods is a poet, playwright and broadcaster. His plays include *At the Black Pig's Dyke*, *A Cry from Heaven* and *Song of the Yellow Bittern*; and plays for radio include *Broken Moon* and *The Gospels of Aughamore*. He has published two collections of poems, *The Colour of Language* and *Lives and Miracles* and co-edited *The Turning Wave: Poems and Songs of Irish Australia*. His song lyrics have been set to music and recorded by many singers in Ireland and the USA. He regularly performs with musicians and singers and a DVD of *The Leitrim Equation 4* concerts is available. He is a well-known broadcaster and has presented many arts programmes and documentaries on RTÉ Radio 1. Vincent was writer-in-residence at NUI Galway where he taught creative writing. He has written a study of poetry and the Great Famine, *Leaves of Hungry Grass*, part of a series of folio publications published by the Great Hunger museum at Quinnipiac University, Connecticut. He lives in Dublin and is a member of Aosdána.

Artisan House

Artisan House is a publishing company creating beautifully illustrated high-quality books and bespoke publications on a richly diverse range of subjects including food and lifestyle, photography and the visual arts, music and poetry.

Creative Director, Vincent Murphy, and Editorial Director, Mary Ruddy, established Artisan House in 2013.

Publications include:

Celebrating Irish Salmon by Máirín Uí Chómain
Joe Boske The Works by Joe Boske
Connemara by Dorothy Cross
Sea Gastronomy: Fish & Shellfish of the North Atlantic by Michael O'Meara; (winner of Best Seafood Cookbook in the World Gourmand Cookbook Awards 2016 and McKennas Guides Cookbook of the Year 2015)
The Mountain Ash broadside by Joan McBreen & Margaret Irwin
An Art Lover's Guide to the French Riviera by Patrick J Murphy
Connemara & Aran by Walter Pfeiffer

Artisan House is a member of Publishing Ireland, Foilsiú Éireann.

Books of *taste*
Created with *passion*
In the heart of *Connemara*

www.artisanhouse.ie